WOMEN'S RIGHTS

Also available in the Small Guides to Big Issues

Climate Change
Melanie Jarman

Cities
Jeremy Seabrook

Small Guides To Big Issues

Geraldine Terry

WOMEN'S RIGHTS

palgrave
macmillan

Fernwood Publishing
Halifax and Winnipeg

First published 2007 by Pluto Press, 345 Archway Road, London N6 5AA, UK
and 839 Greene Street, Ann Arbor, MI 48106, USA. www.plutobooks.com

Published in Australia by Palgrave Macmillan Publishers Australia, Claremont
Street, South Yarra 3141, Australia. Associated companies and representatives
throughout the world. Visit our website at www.macmillan.com.au

Published in Canada by Fernwood Publishing, Site 2A, Box 5, 32 Oceanvista Lane,
Black Point, Nova Scotia, B0J 1B0 and 324 Clare Avenue, Winnipeg, Manitoba,
R3L 1S3. www.fernwoodpublishing.ca

Published in South Africa by Jacana Media (Pty) Ltd, 10 Orange Street,
Sunnyside, Auckland Park 2092, South Africa, tel +2711 628 3200.
See a complete list of Jacana titles at www.jacana.co.za

Published in association with Oxfam GB

The views expressed are those of the author, and not necessarily those of the
publishing organisations.

ISBN	978 0 7453 2349 7 (Pluto hardback)
ISBN	978 0 7453 2348 0 (Pluto paperback)
ISBN	978 1 4202 5602 4 (Palgrave Macmillan)
ISBN	978 1 55266 251 9 (Fernwood)
ISBN	978 1 77009 378 2 (Jacana)

British Library Cataloguing in Publication Data. A catalogue record for this book
is available from the British Library

Library of Congress Cataloging in Publication Data applied for

National Library of Australia cataloguing in publication data applied for

Library and Archives Canada Cataloguing in Publication:
Terry, Geraldine, 1954-
        Women's rights / Geraldine Terry.
(Small guides to big issues)
Includes bibliographical references.
ISBN 978-1-55266-251-9

        1. Women's rights. 2. Sex discrimination against women.
3. Women--Violence against. I. Title. II. Series.
HQ1236.T47 2007   305.42   C2007-903296-6

10 9 8 7 6 5 4 3 2 1

Designed and produced for Pluto Press by Curran Publishing Services, Norwich

Printed and bound in India

Contents

	Series preface	*vi*
	Acknowledgements	*viii*
	List of boxes	*ix*
	List of abbreviations	*xii*
1.	Interconnections	1
2.	Women's human rights: a closer look	24
3.	The threat of cultural relativism	41
4.	'Not a fax from heaven'	51
5.	The podium and the polling booth	64
6.	Women's economic rights in a globalising world	81
7.	'Sowing a seed': the right to education	101
8.	The violence against women pandemic	121
9.	Women's rights abuses help to spread HIV/AIDS	137
10.	The future is already happening	152
	Resources	*163*
	Notes	*176*
	Bibliography	*190*
	Index	*192*

Series Preface

Facts, opinions, and ideas in the fight to end poverty

Small Guides to Big Issues is a series of accessible introductions to key current global challenges.

Books in this series raise bold questions about the global economic and political system, and about how it works. They set out what needs to happen in order to end poverty and injustice. They are designed for campaigners and activists, for students and researchers, in fact for anyone interested in looking behind the headlines.

Each book is informed by personal knowledge and passion and is written in an accessible and thought-provoking style. Each book provides a critical survey of its subject and a challenging look at current trends and debates. Authors explain the global institutions and processes involved, and tackle key issues of poverty reduction, human rights and sustainable development.

The books contain case studies, analysis, and testimony from activists and development practitioners, many drawing on Oxfam's experience of working with partner organisations in more than 70 countries. Oxfam is supporting this series by asking writers with a personal on-the-ground knowledge of the issues to share their view of the key debates in each subject.

Oxfam GB

Oxfam GB, founded in 1942, is a development, humanitarian and campaigning agency working with others worldwide to find lasting solutions to poverty and suffering. Oxfam GB is a member of Oxfam International, a confederation of 13 organisations around the world working for an end to injustice and poverty. Oxfam is committed to making poverty-focused information and analysis of global issues more widely available, and is working in partnership with Pluto Press on this series in order to contribute to current debates. For clarity, the books in this series do not differentiate between Oxfam International or Oxfam GB, or regional offices or affiliate organisations – choosing rather to use 'Oxfam' to cover any or all of these institutions.

Pluto Press

Pluto Press is an independent, progressive, London-based publisher specialising in books on politics and across the social sciences that offer a radical counterpoint to the mainstream. Recent titles address some of the most pressing and contentious issues today, including the economic and ecological impact of globalisation, global insecurity and terrorism, and international human rights.

Acknowledgements

Particular thanks (in no particular order) to:

Jake Grout-Smith and Rebecca Gowland, who both helped to research Oxfam projects; Caroline Sweetman, Sheila Aikman, Sandy Ruxton, Mona Mehta, Shipra Jha, Jenny Enarsson and Kate Raworth of Oxfam GB, Erika Paez of Womankind Worldwide, Timothy Connor of Oxfam Australia, Brooke Hutchinson of CAMFED International, Lesley Anne Foster of Masimanyane Women's Support Centre, Maitrayee Mukhopadhyay of the Royal Tropical Institute, the Netherlands, Pun Ngai of the Chinese Working Women's Network, Simon Moore and Gill Gordon of International HIV/AIDS Alliance, Eno-Obong Akpan, David Archer of ActionAid International and Jyoti Sangh of the We Can campaign, who all provided information and/or advice and comments; Cassandra Balchin of Women Living Under Muslim Laws, Heather Grady of the Ethical Globalisation Initiative, Rose Gawaya of Oxfam, Ann Elisabeth Samson of the Association for Women's Rights in Development and Ulrike Röhr of Genanet, who were good enough to take the time to give me interviews, and, in Cassandra's case, also gave very helpful comments.

List of Boxes

1.1   Some facts and figures   1
1.2   Laying down the law to defy a 'witch-hunt'   2
1.3   Paying lip service to women's emancipation   6
1.4   The Millennium Development Goals   8
1.5   The human development approach   9
1.6   The unequal sexual division of labour   11
1.7   Consumerism, dowry violence and
      sex-selective abortions in India   13
1.8   The collective dimension of empowerment   15
1. 9 The Women's Skill Creation Centre, Nepal   16
1.10 Extract from a speech by Everjoice Win,
      Zimbabwean development worker and activist   18
1.11 Oxfam International and the rights-based
      approach   19

2.1   Key treaties and conferences for women's
      human rights   28
2.2   Re-laying the foundation for women's
      human rights   32
2.3   Women's rights protocol added to the
      African charter   33
2.4   Women hardly figure in UN 'Special
      Procedures' on human rights   35
2.5   Questioning the usefulness of women's
      human rights   37
2.6   Human rights 'less shiny' than before   38

3.1   Girls' Early Marriage in Nigeria   44

3.2	Globalisation and change in Bangladesh	46
3.3	Feminists in the global South: 'Westernised'?	48
4.1	Death by vigilantes	52
4.2	Catholics for a Free Choice	54
4.3	The global gag rule	55
4.4	The diversity of Muslim women	57
4.5	Siti Musdah Mulia, a tool for Western concepts?	58
4.6	Interview with Cassandra Balchin	59
5.1	Achievements of a woman mayor in Ecuador	67
5.2	Limitations of women's political representation	68
5.3	Women taking part in politics in Mali	69
5.4	An Islamic fundamentalist view	71
5.5	Involving women in Afghanistan's elections	71
5.6	Overcoming women's disenfranchisement in Guatemala	74
5.7	Rwanda leads the world on women MPs	76
6.1	What is globalisation?	82
6.2	Women in Angola's informal sector	87
6.3	Women's income as a proportion of men's, by region	88
6.4	How dumping impacts on women farmers in Africa and Central America	91
6.5	Conditions in a Chinese factory with a rush job	94
6.6	Helping women in Chile's informal sector to organise	97
7.1	Number of primary-school-age children out of school by sex and region, 2001/02	102
7.2	Truancy in reverse in Nigeria	105
7.3	Human development gains from girls' education	106
7.4	Waramatou's story	107

7.5	What keeps girls out of school?	108
7.6	'They can only afford to pay for one'	109
7.7	Negative stereotypes in Pakistan's school books	111
7.8	Danger and harassment at school	112
7.9	Small-scale NGO initiatives on girls' education	115
7.10	'Information is power'	117
7.11	'Things began to change'	118
8.1	Small glimpses of a big picture: figures on domestic violence	122
8.2	Violence against women through the life-cycle	123
8.3	Sexual harassment at work	125
8.4	Women's organisations countering violence against women	127
8.5	'Our strength is not for hurting'	128
8.6	Rape as a weapon of war in the Congo	130
9.1	Figures on HIV/AIDS	138
9.2	Women's human rights issues linked to HIV/AIDS in sub-Saharan Africa	140
9.3	The bitter truth about sugar daddies	141
9.4	Marriage may be no protection	143
9.5	Widows lack property rights	143
9.6	The practice of 'sexual cleansing'	144
9.7	Girls' education is a weapon against HIV/AIDS	147

List of Abbreviations

AMME	Association for Gender and Education
AVV	Asociación Aurora Vivar
AWID	Association for Women's Rights in Development
BBC	British Broadcasting Corporation
BPFA	Beijing Platform for Action
CAMFED	Campaign for Female Education
CEDAW	Convention for the Elimination of Discrimination against Women
CFFC	Catholics for a Free Choice
COICAPEP	Coordination of Indigenous Peasant Community Committees for the Promotion and Education for Peace
COVA	Confederation of Voluntary Associations
DAWN	Development Alternatives for Women in the New Era
EU	European Union
FAWE	Federation of African Women Educationalists
FGM	Female genital mutilation
FLAC	Free Legal Aid Committee
GCE	Global Campaign for Education
GSBI	Gabungan Serikat Buruh Independen (an Indonesian trades union)
ICC	International Criminal Court
ICCPR	International Covenant on Civil and Political Rights
ICESCR	International Covenant on Economic, Social and Cultural Rights

ILO	International Labour Organisation
IMF	International Monetary Fund
IPU	Inter-Parliamentary Union
MDGs	Millennium Development Goals
MP	Member of Parliament
NAFTA	North American Free Trade Agreement
NGO	Non-governmental organisation
OCAA	Oxfam Community Aid Abroad (now Oxfam Australia)
OMAFES	Œuvre malienne d'aide à la Femme et à l'enfant au Sahel
PADV	Project against Domestic Violence
PSI	Population Services International
UDHR	Universal Declaration of Human Rights
UK	United Kingdom
UN	United Nations
UNAIDS	Joint United Nations Programme on HIV/AIDS
UNDP	United Nations Development Programme
UNESCO	United Nations Education, Scientific and Cultural Organization
UNHCR	United Nations High Commissioner for Human Rights
UNICEF	United Nations Emergency Fund for Children
UNIFEM	United Nations Development Fund for Women
USA	United States of America
USAID	United States Agency for International Development
VVF	vesico-vaginal fistulae
WAF	Women Against Fundamentalisms
WHO	World Health Organization
WIDE	Women in Development Europe
WLUML	Women Living Under Muslim Laws
WRC	White Ribbon Campaign
WTO	World Trade Organization

1
Interconnections

This book is about the interlocked issues of women's human rights, world poverty and international development. There are different ways of looking at poverty but, however it is defined, it is generally accepted that the majority of poor people across the world are women. Discrimination against women drastically limits their life-chances, and is a brake on development in the global South. Changing this status quo should be at the heart of the development process, and this means helping women to exercise their rights.

Box 1.1: Some facts and figures[1]

- Up to 100 million females are missing from the global population, victims of sex-selective abortion and infant neglect.
- Of the estimated 1.1 billion poor people in the world, an estimated 60–70 per cent are women.
- It is estimated that a woman dies every minute as a result of problems in pregnancy and childbirth; most of these deaths are in the global South, and the vast majority are avoidable.
- Two-thirds of the world's illiterate adults are women.
- Violence against women is one of the biggest causes of deaths and disability among women aged 15–44.
- Women hold only 17 per cent of parliamentary seats worldwide.

Box 1.2: Laying down the law to defy a 'witch-hunt'

Seema and Sukarmani, from a village in Jharkhand, India, have been lifelong friends. A few years ago, they joined a local non-governmental organisation (NGO), the Free Legal Aid Committee (FLAC). They took an active part in FLAC's activities, such as using drama to tackle social concerns like dowry, trafficking in women and the phenomenon of 'witch-hunting'.

In their part of India, economic pressures are reducing access to the agricultural land and forests that people depend on, and powerful men are tightening their control over natural resources. In some communities, this has been accompanied by 'witch-hunts'; there have been several murders of women accused of witchcraft in the last few years. According to Indian rights groups, these 'witch-hunts' are actually motivated by the desire of local priests, tribal chiefs or relatives to get their hands on widows' and divorcees' property.

One day, her neighbour denounced Seema's widowed mother as a witch, blaming her for the fact that his wife had just given birth to a third daughter, instead of a hoped-for son. The village council ordered Seema's mother to be exorcised by the local shaman. Seema knew her mother was too old and frail to withstand the physical manhandling and emotional strain of exorcism; she appealed to Sukarmani for help. On the day appointed for the exorcism, Seema publicly opposed the council. Sukarmani stood by her and threatened to file a case under the Prevention of Witch Practices Act, a law that mandates a year in prison and a fine of 2,000 rupees for anyone who makes an accusation of witchcraft or takes part in torturing women branded as witches.

> Today, the two women are still amazed at their own courage in 'laying down the law' to the council. They say their strength came from the fact they knew they were in the right. Now that they have made their voices heard, they believe other women will also find the courage to stand up for themselves.[2]

ween the facts and figures in Box 1.1
nd Sukarmani in Box 1.2; women's
of the statistics in Box 1.1 represents
women's human rights on a massive
omen have rights in all these areas,
of international human rights agree-
ntries, domestic legislation. When I
ory of these two young women, it
efiance illustrates what development
marginalised women feeling strong
disadvantages, to use their rights as a
injustice together.

ts: a key to development

omen, whether direct or indirect, is one
orces in the world today. It causes vast
d is a major brake on development. In
try to show how the scandal of mass
day's most pressing issues, such as the
e bound up with the denial and abuse of
The focus will be on the global South
high and middle-income countries; by
world's low-income countries. This does
women in affluent parts of the world,
obal North, are free from discrimination,

but that is not what this book is about. Neither do I want to lump together all women in the global South and imply they are all poor. All women encounter discrimination on the grounds of their sex, but there are a lot of other factors, such as their class, race, ethnic group, age, caste, sexual orientation and so on, that combine to shape their particular experience, and they may be privileged in other ways. So the focus is specifically on poor women in the global South.

In this chapter, I will outline how thinking on poverty and development has changed over the last few decades. The most progressive development-aid organisations now support poor women's empowerment, rather than just addressing the material dimensions of their poverty. At the same time, organisations like Oxfam now focus on poor people's rights when they work on eliminating poverty. Chapter 2 briefly charts the development of women's human rights, in the shape of international treaties and agreements. It also gives some examples of how feminist activists in the global South have been able to use this international legislation, and the ideas that inspire it, as tools in their work for justice. Chapters 3 and 4 look at two explicit challenges to the foundational principle that human rights are universal and apply to all women alike: so-called 'cultural relativism', and the rise of fundamentalisms. Chapters 5–9 cover different areas of women's human rights and how their rights are being denied or abused. Chapter 5 is about women's right to take part in politics, Chapter 6 looks at women's economic rights in relation to today's trade system, Chapter 7 is about girls' and women's right to a meaningful and empowering education, Chapter 8 looks at the pandemic of violence against women, and Chapter 9 outlines how this is helping HIV/AIDS to proliferate, with particular reference to sub-Saharan Africa. In Chapter 10, I talk to specialists about two phenomena that are likely to have a huge impact on women's human rights in the coming decades: the development of new technologies that, among other things, are redefining how human beings are

for them, poverty means ill health and premature death, lack of access to education and other basic services, social exclusion, having no say in major decisions that affect them, and vulnerability to harassment, injury and violence. There are also debilitating and distressing psycho-social dimensions, such as a chronic sense of low self-esteem, and social humiliation.[11] Recognising all this, the United Nations Development Programme (UNDP) has pioneered a broader approach to development than the purely economic one that dominated development thinking during the 1980s; at its centre is the idea of 'human development' (Box 1.5).

The human development approach is based on the work of Nobel laureate Amartya Sen. It is multi-dimensional, concentrates on ends (what people want from their lives) rather than means (such as money), and recognises that there is no automatic link between economic growth and human well-being. It helps us to analyse how poor women in the global South are particularly disadvantaged in relation even to poor men in their own societies. They face the same restrictions and adversities, caused by unjust international trade policies, global warming, poor natural resources, ethnic discrimination, armed conflict and so on. But on top of all that, they also have to contend with systematic discrimination against them as women. That discrimination means they

Box 1.5: The human development approach

'The basic purpose of development is to enlarge people's choices. ... People often value achievements that do not show up at all, or not immediately, in income or growth figures: greater access to knowledge, better nutrition and health services, more secure livelihoods, security against crime and physical violence, satisfying leisure hours, political and cultural freedoms and a sense of participation in community activities. The objective of development is to create an enabling environment for people.'[12]

experience all these phenomena in different ways from men, and it limits their options even further.

For instance, millions of poor women throughout Africa and South Asia are prevented by traditional custom and law from owning land, however hard they work on it to grow food for their families. This deprives them of choices such as how to use the land, whether to branch out into new business ventures, apply for a loan using the land as collateral and so on. It makes it harder for them to climb out of the poverty trap than it is for men in their communities, for whom such options are available. Poor women's 'achievements', to use the UNDP's term, are also restricted, for instance by the denial of a decent education, or because they are subject to routine domestic violence that saps their health, confidence, self-esteem and energy. One of the most important factors of all is the unequal sexual division of labour (Box 1.6). Many cultures put the entire burden of bringing up children, looking after sick relatives, fetching water, cooking and cleaning on women and girls, leaving them very little time for what the UNDP calls 'satisfying leisure hours'; in other words, they are 'time-poor' as well as poor in material terms. Seeing development in terms of well-being, choices and what people can do with their lives, rather than a purely economic process, helps to show why women should be at the heart of development aid initiatives.

The unequal division of labour starts at childhood. In many countries in the global South, it is common to see groups of young boys playing in the street, while girls are nowhere to be seen; they are indoors, helping their mothers to cook, clean and look after younger siblings. In June 2005, I spoke to groups of teenage boys and girls in schools in a rural area of The Gambia in West Africa. They told me that the girls' days start two hours earlier than the boys'. They have to get up earlier than everyone else so they can fetch water and start cooking breakfast for the rest of the family. When they get to school things are not much different, because most of the school housekeeping tasks, such as cleaning the classrooms, fall to girls, while the boys 'sit under

Box 1.6: The unequal sexual division of labour

One of the commonest 'poverty' images we see in fundraising materials and on TV is women and girls trudging off to fetch water. All over the global South, this task falls to females, and for thousands, perhaps millions, of women and girls, it can take them several hours of walking each day. In her village in western Pakistan, 42-year-old Jamal Khatoon used to get up at 6 every morning and walk to a spring 6 kilometres away, up in the mountains. She is married, with four daughters and two sons:

> I was the only one to wake up in the early morning and prepare my donkey to fetch 80 litres of water for my family. After two hours I reached the spring and filled four 20-litre containers. Then I went back to my house to prepare lunch for my family and look after my children. ... When I reached home my children were weeping from hunger and it crushed my spirit.[13]

Oxfam has now installed a pump in the village, a huge benefit for both Jamal and her family.

a tree and watch'. After school, the boys play football while the girls wash dishes and sweep floors. Exhausted, girls go to bed two hours earlier than the boys, so they can get up early and start all over again the next day.

Focusing on women's empowerment

Although the human development approach is very helpful in analysing how poor women are more disadvantaged than poor men in the global South, it stops short of explaining why this is so. Essentially it is a 'technical' way of analysing poverty and well-being, not a political one. This is where power and empowerment come in. Inequalities in power help to create and perpetuate poverty. This is true for inequalities between men and women, as well as between rich and poor people, or different ethnic groups. Because, while poor men in the global South lack power in many ways, in general they can still wield it over women and children in their households and communities. I am not arguing here that all poor men are domestic tyrants, or that all poor women are 'victims' of men, only that many societies in the global South are characterised by severe power imbalances between the sexes. This means that increased wealth does not necessarily bring more choices and achievements for women; just think about oil-rich Saudi Arabia, where even women from wealthy families are not allowed to drive. Figures compiled by the NGO Social Watch bear this point out; they show that there is no automatic relationship between a country's wealth and gender equity, although it is true that most of the countries where women's status is good are also among the richest nations.[14] Where power is overwhelmingly in men's hands rather than women's, greater affluence can actually cause harm to women and girls. This seems to be happening in India, where commentators see links between increasing consumerism, dowry violence and the widespread practice of aborting female foetuses (see Box 1.7).[15] There is an important lesson here: women in the global South need more than economic growth and increased wealth.

If poor women's deprivation is a matter of grossly unequal power relations, then it follows that the process of 'empowerment' should be integral to development efforts. As with many other terms in development aid, not everyone means the same thing when they use the word, but it is generally accepted that it has something to do with a person's ability to take some control over her or his own life. There are different types of power. As well as the nakedly visible power exercised by large

Box 1.7: Consumerism, dowry violence and sex-selective abortions in India

Every six hours in India, a young married woman is burned alive, beaten to death or driven to commit suicide because of India's illegal but rampant dowry system. Back in history, dowry began as gifts of land to a woman as her inheritance in an essentially agricultural economy. But Malavika Rajkotia, a lawyer specialising in women's issues, says that in today's increasingly consumerist society many husbands and their parents try to squeeze more dowry out of their wives in order to satisfy consumer needs, and are prepared to use violence.[16] In urban middle-class households, demands can include a house, car and large sums of cash. In 2003, 21-year-old Nisha Sharma, a software engineer in Delhi, became headline news. On her wedding day, she had her prospective bridegroom arrested because he had suddenly demanded an extra $25,000 in dowry, and physically threatened her father. She became a role model for many middle-class Indian women across the country, and in the days that followed several other brides took similar action.[17] But the systematic use of violence to extract dowry from wives' families continues, with murders of young married women often passed off by in-laws as 'stove accidents'.

Excessive dowry demands can mean impoverishment and indebtedness for poor families with daughters, and can go on well into the marriage. Dowries have become such a burden that many families are desperate to avoid having female children. While the statistics on dowry deaths are chilling, so too is India's dismal sex ratio. Data from India's 2001 census shows the sex ratio for children aged six and under fell from 945 females per 1,000 males in 1991 (already unnaturally low) to just 927 in 2001. This compares with a global statistical norm of 1,050 females for every 1,000 males. The disturbing trend is largely due to the practice of using ultrasound scans to identify female foetuses, and then aborting them. According to the Campaign against Female Foeticide, 90 per cent of the estimated 3.5 million abortions in India each year are to eliminate girls.[18] Sex-selective abortions are by no means confined to poor families. According to Usha Rai, Deputy Director of the Press Institute of India, in 2000 the sex ratio of new-born babies in the most prosperous part of Delhi was down to a mere 845 girls for every 1,000 boys.[19]

companies, governments and some individuals, there are subtler forms, such as widely-held cultural assumptions about women's inferiority compared to men. For instance, a World Bank report on Zambia notes how some traditional sayings there, such as 'Is a woman a human being?', express the commonly-held idea that women are worth less than men.[20]

Many women unconsciously accept such ideas; this is not surprising, as they have been drummed into them since childhood. For instance, when CARE-Malawi staff spoke to village women about their rights, they noticed that none of the women mentioned the domestic violence that is rife in their communities. The researchers commented: 'women may have internalised feeling of blame and/or not feel free to speak out.'[21] Helping such women to realise they have 'a right to have rights', such as the right not to be physically abused by their partners, is an important step towards them feeling empowered. There are also collective, as well as individual, dimensions to empowerment, as feminist academic Naila Kabeer describes (see Box 1.8).

Many small NGOs in the global South are supporting poor

Box 1.8: The collective dimension of empowerment[22]

From a state of powerlessness that manifests itself in a feeling of 'I cannot', empowerment contains an element of collective self-confidence that results in a feeling of 'we can'.

women's empowerment through their projects. In Latin America, there is a strong tradition of working alongside poor men and women in consciousness-raising activities, based on the seminal work of Paulo Freire in the 1960s and 1970s. In India, there is a different, but very vibrant, tradition of grassroots activism, which the story in Box 1.2 illustrates. Many of Oxfam's partner organisations combine practical activities for women, like skills-training, micro-credit and literacy, with raising awareness about rights and discussing important issues such as domestic violence. The idea is that women involved in these activities will become agents for positive change, rather than passive recipients of top-down 'development'; see Box 1.9, on the work of the Women's Skill Creation Centre in Nepal.

The rights-based approach to development

The account in Box 1.9 is just one of many 'women's empowerment' success stories. This kind of strategy can have great impact at individual and community levels, but can only go so far in challenging deep power imbalances. Recognising this, in recent years development agencies such as Oxfam and the UK's Department for International Development have made human rights the guiding principle for their work. This reflects the agendas of many civil society organisations and social movements in the global South. The rights-based approach comes from an essentially political understanding of development, based on analysing cross-cutting inequalities among different

Box 1.9: The Women's Skill Creation Centre, Nepal

In Nepal, the figures for maternal mortality, life expectancy and educational achievement all show that women have very low status. Oxfam's partner organisations in Nepal work with poor men and women to raise their awareness of issues like trafficking in women, violence against women and the role of women in decision making.[23] Bishnu Ojha is President of the Women's Skill Creation Centre in Basamadi village, Hetauda:

> We held literacy classes and trained the women in tailoring and fabric painting to make them more self-reliant. But time and again we came across women unaware of their basic rights and affected by domestic violence – so we started to raise their awareness of HIV/AIDS, domestic violence and human rights.

A member of the group sums up how she has changed through these activities: 'In the beginning I had lost my willpower and thought I could do nothing. Until recently I didn't leave my home. But now, I feel confident and am aware of my rights.'

The women are being encouraged to take on positions of influence in the community. According to another member of the group, Menuka Paudel: 'Women weren't interested in politics before. But with the help of Oxfam and the Women's Skill Creation Centre we know what our rights are, and how to use them.' Several women in the group now have plans to stand in local and district elections, which they would never have contemplated before getting involved with the Centre.

classes, races, ethnic groups and men and women, as well as a range of other factors that distinguish groups of people from one another. It is quite different from economic or technical approaches that see development as a benign process where the rich world helps the poor world to 'catch up'; in these types of approach, the political nature of development tends to be understated or ignored. In the rights-based approach, human rights are tools that poor men and women can use to bring about improved social justice.

Accountability – the principle that parties such as governments and large companies have a duty to uphold people's rights – is central to human rights thinking. This idea that you can legitimately demand action from national and local government, companies and other bodies is what gives human rights much of their strength. For poor women, just realising they have certain rights can be, in itself, empowering. It is unlikely that Seema and Sukarmani (Box 1.2) would have felt strong enough to challenge the village council if they had not known that Seema's mother was protected by law, thanks to the organisation they belonged to.

In Box 1.10, Everjoice Win vividly describes how women in the global South are often shown in development literature; most of us are familiar with the kind of image she is talking about. Taking a rights perspective on women's poverty in the global South changes our perceptions. We realise that poor women are not helpless charity cases but claimants of justice, not 'beneficiaries' of development aid, but agents for positive change. Instead of focusing on their 'needs', we think in terms of their entitlements. A rights approach also means analysing how national and international policies and structures, such as trade arrangements, impact on poor women and men, and campaigning for change where these policies cause harm. This is because, without changes at the macro-level, working towards empowerment at the level of villages and households can only have limited success. For instance, Asociación Aurora

Box 1.10: Extract from a speech by Everjoice Win, Zimbabwean development worker and activist[24]

'I want to put on the table a discussion about who the woman in development is. Who is the woman on the covers of our books? Why do we have that image of poor, powerless and pregnant or with a child on her back or pulling behind her, heavily laden etc., and why is this image of women so enduring?

Vivar, the Peruvian organisation whose work is featured at the end of this chapter, combines empowerment and rights-training programmes for low-income women with national and regional campaigning.

For development agencies like Oxfam, focusing on poor women's and men's rights is a strategy for achieving development. Others argue that men and women fulfilling their human rights *is* development. Putting that debate about ends and means aside, the important thing is that the trend towards rights-based development is well under way. It represents a partial convergence of two traditions, 'development' and 'human rights', which have until recently been separate. This drawing-together can only be a good thing, not least because each side can complement and learn from the other. On the level of international development policy, the UN sees the Millennium Development Goals, especially MDG3, as a way of integrating the human rights and development policy agendas.[25]

The story at the end of this chapter looks at how the work of a women's organisation in Peru, Asociación Aurora Vivar, has evolved from practical skills training for women to lobbying, campaigning and awareness-raising for women's economic rights, such as their rights to decent and secure work.

Box 1.11: Oxfam International and the rights-based approach

Oxfam International is a confederation of 13 organisations working together to fight poverty and injustice around the world. They share a global strategic plan and pursue joint efforts in campaigning and programming. Between them they support more than 3000 counterpart organisations in approximately 100 countries. Heather Grady is a former East Asia Regional Director for Oxfam GB.[26] I asked her why Oxfam decided to adopt a rights-based approach to its work:

G.T. Oxfam is well known as an organisation dedicated to eliminating poverty. When did it become concerned with rights, and why?

H.G. The formal decision to adopt a rights-based approach was made in 2000. It was entirely in keeping with Oxfam's mission of ending unnecessary poverty and suffering, because Oxfam defines poverty as a state of powerlessness in which people are denied their human rights and the ability to control crucial aspects of their lives. Previous approaches, such as focusing on basic needs or promoting sustainable livelihoods, had only limited success. With a rights-based approach, Oxfam hopes to transform vicious circles of poverty so that poor people can demand account-ability from governments, transnational companies and others.

G.T. Can you give an example of how the rights-based approach works in practice?

H.G. At the international level, Oxfam supports campaigns such as Make Trade Fair and Make Poverty History.

They're designed to spur citizens in the rich North to hold their own governments accountable for policies that are widening the gap between rich and poor. Oxfam also supports organisations in the global South to lobby and campaign for the promotion and protection of rights.

Let me give you an example: Oxfam worked with poor cotton farmers in the Sahel region of Africa to help them voice their views at the World Trade Organization meeting in Cancun, Mexico, in 2003. They called attention to how subsidised cotton from the United States was being dumped on world markets, damaging their livelihoods. It contributed to a groundswell against the subsidies, and eventually the World Trade Organization declared them to be contrary to its rules.

G.T.   How easily have Oxfam staff and partner organisations taken the new rights-based approach on board? Are there any outstanding challenges?

H.G.   As with any NGO, Oxfam sometimes finds it difficult to translate theory into practice in all its programmes. On the positive side, Oxfam has substantial experience in working on issues from the local level upwards, building people's understanding and skills in relation to rights and linking organisations at different levels, and these are all important elements of a rights-based approach.

From mending irons to demanding rights

Peru is one of the poorest countries in South America. Events in the 1990s, including structural adjustment, the international financial crisis and natural disasters, combined with corruption, political instability and terrorism to produce high levels of poverty and deprivation. An estimated 49 per cent of the Peruvian population are categorised as poor, of whom about half are officially classified as living in extreme poverty. Against this backdrop, Peruvian women still earn only 80 per cent of what men earn, domestic violence is endemic and women are marginalised from politics; only 18 per cent of seats in the Peruvian Congress are held by women.

It was in this context that women's NGO Asociación Aurora Vivar (AVV) began its Alternative Technical Training Programme in the early 1990s. It is interesting to see how its work has changed since then. From a reliance on traditional 'development' strategies for tackling women's poverty, it now embraces a rights-based approach. AVV's vision is a culture where women and men realise they 'have a right to have rights', as well as having the practical skills to survive in a harsh economic climate.

At first, AVV decided to enhance the entrepreneurial skills of unemployed and low-income women in the shanty towns of Lima. By training them to repair household appliances such as irons and fridges, combined with courses in leadership skills, confidence building and business management, the organisation hoped to meet these women's immediate needs for paid work. Challenging macho stereotypes about what type of work women can and cannot do was also an important element.

But the organisation soon realised that the women trainees knew little or nothing of their economic rights, so it decided to provide training in that too. The women who run Peru's community kitchens were an important target group. There is a big network of such kitchens throughout Lima; women started them up during a period of economic and political crisis, when economic austerity was throwing thousands out of work, and the savagery of the guerrilla movement Sendero Luminoso ('Shining Path') was compounding the sense of chaos. The kitchens were a useful way to show solidarity with unemployed men and their families. People contributed whatever food they had, as well as help with cooking and cleaning, and women who worked in the kitchens got free meals for themselves and their families. There is now a federation of community kitchens with elected leaders, and their role has expanded.

According to Alejandrina Rosaria Flores Coya, a volunteer director with one of the kitchens, 'As well as helping to feed families when times are hard, we are interested in helping women grow in all aspects of their lives.' AVV runs training programmes where the volunteers learn about their economic, cultural and social rights, for instance the right to fair treatment by employers or decent housing, discuss how these relate to women and their communities, and find practical ways to measure progress. The training provides tools that low-income women can use in their struggles through the community kitchens and trade unions.

Realising that training can only have a limited impact on its own, AVV also engages in lobbying, campaigning and communications at different levels. It had a recent success in the Ica region where, working with other NGOs, it persuaded the regional authorities to commit themselves to women's economic rights in their equal opportunities plan. At the national level, its staff and volunteers helped to organise a public tribunal on women's economic and social rights violations in 2005. It has also gone beyond national boundaries by its involvement in the Work, Women and Economy network, which has chapters in eleven countries.[27]

One of AVV's funding partners is WOMANKIND Worldwide, based in the UK. According to Erika Paez, their Central and Latin America Programme Manager:

> AVV's training is very effective, but the organisation realised it would make a much bigger impact if it could influence the decisions government was making.

Globalisation, in the shape of economic prescriptions from the World Bank, has probably been the biggest factor working against women's economic rights here in Peru. A lot of women have had to take work that is precarious, with few rights of any kind. That makes it much harder for them to organise and work together. But despite globalisation, AVV believes the government still has an important role to play in helping women to realise their economic rights.[28]

What makes AVV's work so interesting is its mix of strategies. Citing international agreements might be rather sterile if it were not, at the same time, building low-income women's ability to demand economic rights for themselves. As Erika Paez points out:

This organisation has been developing its expertise on women's economic rights for over 20 years, and WOMANKIND Worldwide has been working with it for ten. We think that amount of experience is very valuable and should be built on. AVV is quite unusual, because what it is doing straddles both the rights-based and the traditional 'development' approaches to women's poverty. It is showing that there can be a really good synergy between the two.[29]

2
Women's human rights: a closer look

Since the Convention for the Elimination of Discrimination against Women entered into force in 1981, other international agreements have elaborated on women's rights in different areas. However, it is only quite recently that women's human rights have begun to be recognised as an integral element within the human rights tradition. Despite weaknesses in the international legislation, and the ever-present threat that hostile governments will claw back what has been won at the international level, women's organisations all over the world use these agreements in their lobbying and campaigning against gender inequality.

> Human rights are inscribed in the hearts of people; they were there long before lawmakers drafted their first proclamation.
>
> Mary Robinson, former United Nations High Commissioner for Human Rights[1]

What do we mean by 'rights'?

For many of us, the idea that people have rights is something we take for granted, perhaps without thinking too much about it. But what exactly do we mean when we talk about rights? Rights exist on different levels. Legally speaking, they are embodied n national legislation and international treaties such as the Universal Declaration of Human Rights. But human rights are more than just legal matters. More broadly, a human right is a legitimate claim that an individual has on others, whether these 'others' are individuals, groups, societies or nation states, which the 'others' have a duty to respond to. According to this view, it reflects a basic commitment to human solidarity. A third, more pragmatic view of rights is that they are legal and political tools that can be useful in struggles for social justice.

There are two basic types of human right. Some, such as the right to education, are positive. Governments have a duty to fulfil this type of right, for instance by establishing the appropriate legislation, and providing a decent education system for girls and women. Others are 'negative' rights, such as a women's right not to be subjected to violence from her partner. Governments, as well as other parties such as companies, have a duty to both respect and uphold this type of right. In the case of violence against women, for instance, governments have a duty to refrain from committing such violence themselves through the police and the army. They also have a duty to prevent others from committing violence against women, by legislating against it, enforcing this legislation by prosecuting husbands who attack their wives, running campaigns to raise awareness about domestic violence, and so on.

All this is set out in a range of international human rights treaties. But there is an obvious distinction between having rights in theory and being able to exercise them in practice. So-called negative rights are routinely violated, as in the case of domestic violence or sexual harassment at work. And positive rights are being denied to millions, such as girls denied the right to an education because they are not sent to school. In fact women's human rights are abused and denied so commonly that it is legitimate to wonder if rights have any real significance as far as vast numbers of ordinary women's lives are concerned; women like Jamal Khatoon, whose daily trek for water we read about in the last chapter. I hope to show in this book that they have, and that women like Jamal have as much right to have rights as women in affluent societies.

At this point, you may be wondering if it is legitimate to focus on the denial of *women's* human rights in the context of poverty and development, rather than men's. Of course, men have their rights violated too, but usually due to political, social or ethnic factors that affect both sexes, not because they are men: for instance because they lack bargaining power with an unscrupulous employer or they belong to one of India's 'scheduled' castes. In contrast, many of the rights violations that poor women and girls suffer are, at least in part, because they are female. In Northern Nigeria, for instance, both boys and girls suffer from severe and widespread poverty. However, discrimination against women and girls means that 30 per cent fewer girls than boys enrol in school.[2] As well as suffering human rights violations because they are women, women also experience some that are specific to women in their form. This legal point has been established since the systematic mass rapes and other gender-specific atrocities of civil wars during the 1990s, in countries such as Rwanda and Bosnia.

A second reason why it is valid to focus on women's rights is that violations of women's human rights have often been overlooked by human rights bodies, so it is a way of redressing the balance. Focusing on women's human rights does not necessarily mean excluding men. In fact, there are several examples of campaigns and projects where men are involved in promoting women's human rights, such as the high-profile White Ribbon Campaign to end violence against women; see Chapter 5 for more on this.

The international human rights framework

The idea of human rights is underpinned by a framework of international treaties. They are part of a tradition that is often said to have its roots in the 'Enlightenment' of eighteenth-century Europe. However, Professor Amartya Sen has pointed out that the basic principles of the human rights tradition can also be found in other regions, cultures and periods.[3] The Cyrus Cylinder, made in Babylon in 539 BC, is sometimes called the 'first charter of human rights'. Many important human rights struggles, such as the long and bitter fight against apartheid in South Africa, have happened in the global South, often in the context of anti-colonialism. In 1919, a deputation from the Women's India Association met the British viceroy to demand votes for Indian women at around the same time that suffragists were struggling for women's right to vote in Britain and the United States.

The foundation for human rights was laid in 1948, when the General Assembly of the United Nations proclaimed the Universal Declaration of Human Rights (UDHR), setting out a vision and basic principles. Crucially for women's human rights, Article 2 contains these words: 'Everyone is entitled to all the rights and freedoms set forth in this Declaration, without distinction of any kind'; this included the distinction of sex.[4] Since then, there have been other treaties and declarations elaborating the UDHR. Some cover specific types of right, such as economic and political rights. Others cover particular vulnerable groups, such as children or ethnic minorities. Box 2.1 contains a summary of significant pieces of international legislation and key international conferences. In March 2006, the General Assembly voted to create a new Human Rights Council within the UN system, which is intended to help the UN to address gross and systematic human rights abuses more quickly than in the past.

CEDAW: a women's rights milestone

In 1979, after years of campaigning by feminists, the UN adopted the Convention on the Elimination of All Forms of Discrimination against Women (CEDAW). CEDAW outlaws discrimination against women, and goes further by requiring states that ratify it to take positive steps to end such discrimination, which the convention defines as:

Box 2.1: Key treaties and conferences for women's human rights[5]

Universal Declaration of Human Rights 1948
   Sets out a vision and basic principles.

International Covenant on Civil and Political Rights 1976
   Covers rights such as the right not to be subjected to arbitrary arrest, detention or torture and the right to freedom of conscience and expression. Women and men have equal rights to everything covered in the ICCPR. The ICCPR commits ratifying states to 'take the necessary steps' to put the rights it contains into effect.

International Covenant on Economic, Social and Cultural Rights 1976
   Covers rights such as the right to social security, an adequate standard of living and the highest attainable standard of physical and mental health. Women and men have equal rights to everything covered in the ICESCR. The ICESCR only commits a ratifying country to take steps 'to the maximum of its available resources, with a view to achieving progressively the full realisation' of the rights it contains. It is generally regarded as being weaker than the ICCPR.

Convention for the Elimination of Discrimination against Women 1981
   Sometimes described as 'an international bill of rights for women'. Outlaws discrimination against women, and requires states that ratify it to take positive steps to end such discrimination.

Convention on the Rights of the Child 1990

The Convention defines anyone under the age of 18 years as a child. It has four core principles: non-discrimination; devotion to the best interests of the child; the right to life, survival and development; and respect for the views of the child. By inference, it protects girls from early marriage and harmful traditional practices like female genital mutilation.

World Conference on Human Rights, Vienna 1993

The first of a series of big UN World Conferences during the 1990s which strengthened or clarified different aspects of women's human rights. In a Declaration, the assembled governments affirmed that 'The human rights of women and of the girl-child are an inalienable, integral and indivisible part of universal human rights.'[6]

International Conference on Population and Development, Cairo 1994

Endorsed a new international strategy on population that focused on the needs of individual women and men, rather than concentrating on demographic targets. Focused on supporting women's empowerment and making family planning universally available by 2015.

Fourth World Conference on Women, Beijing 1995

Through a Platform for Action, governments at this conference defined the actions they needed to take in order to realise the rights in CEDAW. The official conference was accompanied by an unprecedented international mobilisation of feminist campaigners and academics from all over the world.

any distinction, exclusion or restriction made on the basis of sex which has the effect or purpose of impairing or nullifying the recognition, enjoyment or exercise by women, irrespective of their marital status, on a basis of equality of men and women, of human rights and fundamental freedoms in the political, economic, social, cultural, civil or any other field.[7]

States that have ratified CEDAW have committed themselves to taking positive action to end discrimination against women. This means incorporating the principle of equality of men and women in their legal systems, abolishing laws that discriminate against women and, if necessary, establishing new ones that make discrimination illegal. They are also obliged to make sure that individuals, organisations or companies do not discriminate against women. At the time of writing, over 90 per cent of UN members are party to the Convention.

But the picture is not as positive as it first seems. Many ratifying countries have registered 'reservations' to CEDAW, meaning that they do not accept certain parts of it. In fact, there are more significant reservations against CEDAW than against any other international human rights treaty. According to Dorcas Coker-Appiah, a Ghanaian women's rights specialist who is on the CEDAW Committee, reservations reflect women's status in the state that makes them.[8] The blizzard of reservations has seriously weakened CEDAW. The UN's Division for the Advancement of Women is particularly concerned about the number of countries that have registered reservations to Articles 2 and 16. Article 2 commits ratifying states to refrain from discriminating against women themselves, and to pursue policies to eliminate discrimination; in other words, it is absolutely central to the Convention. Article 16 covers aspects of marriage and the family, and commits states to eliminate discrimination against women in this sphere; again, it is fundamental to CEDAW. According to the Association for Women's Rights in Development: 'Some of the objections undermine the very purpose of the Convention and are arguably impermissible under international law.'[9]

Despite these problems, women's groups all over the world have found CEDAW useful. For instance, governments that have ratified CEDAW have to submit a report at least every four years, showing what steps they have taken to comply with their treaty obligations. NGOs can submit alternative reports if they think the government does not accurately represent the situation. Women's groups all over the world have seized this opportunity to draw attention to abuses and lobby their governments to take action. At a conference in London to celebrate the 25th anniversary of CEDAW, Shanthi Dairiam of International Women's Rights Action Watch in Kuala Lumpur, also a CEDAW committee member, made the point that women's gains from CEDAW come from using it as a 'hook' to hang lobbying and campaigns on.[10] At the same conference, representatives of women's organisations from countries as diverse as South Africa, Peru and Nepal talked about how they had been able to make use of CEDAW and the rest of the international human rights framework; see the end of this chapter for an example. In 1999 the UN adopted an 'Optional Protocol' which makes it easier to enforce CEDAW in two ways.[11] First, in states that have ratified the Optional Protocol, individual women, or groups of women, can now bring complaints to the Committee, which was not possible before. Second, the Committee can now itself decide to investigate cases where it suspects grave and/or systematic women's rights abuses are happening.

Since CEDAW, there have been other milestones for women's human rights; see Box 2.1. How women's organisations use them depends in part on the political contexts in which they find themselves. Some, like Asociación Aurora Vivar in Peru, explicitly refer to human rights agreements in their lobbying, campaigning and training; in general, the Latin American women's movement is skilled in using human rights legislation, especially regional agreements, to protect and promote women's interests. In other parts of the world, especially where the political environment is hostile to the idea of human rights, women's organisations may use them as a set of guiding principles, an implicit reference point, or perhaps just an inspiration.

Sadly, since the Beijing conference of 1995, women's human rights groups in the North and South have been fragmented and on the defensive. Time and time again, they have had to scramble to stop the gains of the three big 1990s conferences being clawed back by the Vatican and hostile governments. For instance, during the ten-year review of the Beijing Platform for Action (BPFA) in 2005, the Bush government tried, unsuccessfully, to prevent it being reaffirmed without change.[12] Activists were disappointed by *In Larger Freedom: Towards Development, Security and Human Rights For All*, the UN Secretary-General Kofi Annan's report issued in advance of the 2005 World Summit. According to the Women's Environment and Development Organisation, it made no reference to women's rights in the sections on security or human rights. Kathambi Kinoti's comment (Box 2.2) expresses the frustration that many women's rights activists felt at around that time.

On a more positive note, 2005 saw a real step forward in Africa. Following intensive campaigning, the Protocol on the

Box 2.2: Re-laying the foundation for women's human rights

'It seems that [we] have to keep covering and re-covering the same ground. In whatever new sphere of human interest and advancement, the foundation for women's rights has to be laid over and over again, as if it had not been understood in the previous discussion.'

Kathambi Kinoti, Association for Women's Rights in Development

Rights of Women in Africa, a supplement to the African Charter on Human and People's Rights, officially entered into force (Box 2.3).

Box 2.3: Women's rights protocol added to African charter

In October 2005, Togo ratified the Protocol to the African Charter on Human and People's Rights on the Rights of Women. This was the 15th ratification by an African government, and it meant that the protocol could officially enter into force after 30 days. The decision followed a vigorous pan-African campaign by Solidarity for African Women's Rights, involving conferences, press releases and the publication of a booklet, *Not Yet a Force for Freedom*, as well as activities by national women's coalitions all over Africa. I asked Rose Gawaya of Oxfam, who was involved in campaigning for the protocol, why it was important.

R.G.   It's the first legal instrument enshrining the rights of African women. It's indigenous to Africa, unlike CEDAW, which might explain why so many African governments made reservations, based on religion or customary law, when they ratified CEDAW. And the protocol deals with issues specific to African women, such as widow inheritance and female genital mutilation.

G.T.   Now that the protocol has entered into force, is that the end of the campaign you've been involved in?

R.G.   No, there's still a lot of work to be done! Now we have to make sure it is really taken on board by African governments – it has to be domesticated, and put into practice. In some countries it's already happening. For instance, in Zambia, the draft constitution contains most of the contents of the protocol, while South Africa's legal framework already covers most of it.

G.T.   What obstacles do you see ahead of the campaign?

R.G.   Lack of awareness about the protocol is a big challenge. Our research has revealed that even some government officials in women's ministries don't know of the protocol's existence, and even if they have heard of it, they don't know what it says.

G.T.   Can a legal instrument like the protocol really make a difference to poor women's lives in Africa?

R.G.   Obviously it won't make any difference unless it is put into practice. But if it is – and that is what we are going to focus on now – then of course it will change things for the better. For instance, the protocol contains proposals to encourage peace education in schools, which should help to reduce violence against women. It also promotes women's involvement in cultural activities, which is vital, because discrimination against women is reinforced through culture.

Biases and weaknesses

Until recently, the human rights movement failed to recognise a whole range of discriminatory and oppressive practices against women as human rights violations. For instance, according to Article 5 of the UDHR, 'No one shall be subjected to torture or to cruel, inhuman or degrading treatment or punishment,' but it is only recently that either dowry murders in India or female genital mutilation in Africa have started to be seen as human rights issues.[13] Thanks to groundbreaking work by feminists, this mindset is being challenged. For instance, in 2004 Amnesty

International launched a high-profile campaign 'Stop Violence against Women', which among other things calls for domestic violence to be dealt with under UDHR's Article 5, while Human Rights Watch has publicised the epidemic of sexual violence against girls in African schools (see Chapter 6). There is still a long way to go, though, in getting women's human rights into the mainstream; see Box 2.4

Why did the mainstream human rights bodies not see from the start that women's subordination was a human rights issue? The apparent blindness goes back a long way.[14] Historically, the human rights tradition has been preoccupied by civil and political rights abuses perpetrated by governments against their own, male, citizens, such as arbitrary arrest and detention. It has paid much less attention to abuses in the domestic sphere. Although both women and men have their human rights abused by states, it is mainly women (and children) who suffer human rights abuses within families, especially in societies where power is concentrated in fathers, husbands and eldest sons. Women's

Box 2.4: Women hardly figure in UN 'Special Procedures' on human rights

A message circulated by the Quick Response Desk at the Office of the United Nations Commissioner for Human Rights in November 2004 highlighted bias against women in the international rights movement. It drew attention to the fact that, in the first months of 2004, only 10 per cent of human rights 'Special Procedures' concerned women. These special procedures are usually urgent appeals to governments concerning human rights violations, based on information sent by groups and individuals. The message urges women's groups and human rights activists to be more active in observing and reporting human rights abuses against women.[15]

human rights are also abused in other social arenas such as schools and the workplace, often through customs and traditions that are rarely questioned, such as unequal pay. I remember trying to convince a project manager in southern India some years ago that he should pay his female labourers the same as men doing the same work; the interplay of my earnestness and his bafflement was comical. Not so funny, though, for the small, grey-haired woman hefting bricks and sand in front of us while we were talking.

Taking women's human rights violations for granted, as a 'natural' state of affairs, is one reason why they have often been overlooked. In effect, they have been invisible. This also partly explains why it is so difficult for women to actually exercise the rights they possess in theory. Laws are important for promoting changes in social relations, but equal rights on paper mean little if the behaviour and attitudes that so often underlie women's human rights abuses are ignored.[16] The challenge now is to make 'paper rights' real for the millions of women all over the world whose lives are as yet untouched by international agreements. As Shanthi Dairiam notes, women cannot rely on government goodwill to do it.[17]

Of course, the human rights tradition is not the only way to look at women's low status in many parts of the global South; in this complex post-modernist era, no single perspective can suffice for that. In general, the human rights framework is the product of political liberalism, rather than an agenda that sets out to transform power relations. Some feminists argue that the tradition is not very useful when it comes to challenging some of the structural inequalities that hamper women; see the quotation from Ghanaian academic and activist Dodzi Tsikata in Box 2.5. Also, individual agreements and declarations have specific weaknesses. Inexplicably, for instance, CEDAW does not directly refer to violence against women, while the BPFA stresses small-scale interventions such as micro-credit rather than addressing how economic globalisation is affecting women's lives.

Box 2.5: Questioning the usefulness of women's human rights

'Are rights the best analytical tools for understanding and challenging globalisation, militarism, the rise of the transnationals, the impacts of neo-liberal policies, class, gender, race, kinship and other social relations? Does it help us to understand the world trading system? Even marriage and intra-household relations? I think not.'

Dodzi Tsikata[18]

These are certainly weaknesses. All the same, human rights have a powerful resonance with millions of people, and are the product of decades of struggle. It would be foolish not to make use of them in efforts to eliminate the social injustice and poverty that many women in the global South face. In 2003, the 10th Anniversary of the Vienna Conference, an American university polled 146 women's organisations all over the world. Among other things, the organisations were asked how they were using the idea of human rights in their work on violence against women. One replied 'We feel it is empowering for women, action-demanding and compelling to most people – whether men, women, youth, children, professional or non-professionals, it also helps people feel linked with something larger than themselves and legitimises the work for hard-to-convince groups.'[19]

One of the problems with 'rights talk' is that it lends itself to misuse. One of the reasons used by the US government to justify its invasion of Afghanistan in 2001 was its desire to protect women's rights there, although the United States has never ratified CEDAW. The hypocrisy of claiming the moral high ground on rights while running a brutal occupation in Iraq and the so-called 'war on terror', with all the attendant rights abuses in Abu Ghraib prison, Guantanamo Bay and elsewhere, undermines the US government's credibility around promoting rights and has provoked a backlash against the whole project, as Devaki Jain points out (Box 2.6). At the same time, resources that could have been used to further the Millennium Development Goals are being spent on the 'war on terror'; see Cassandra Balchin's comments on this in Chapter 4. For the foreseeable future, this could be the biggest challenge for the rights-based approach, and for women's human rights in particular. Against this backdrop, it might seem an odd time to be arguing that women's human rights are the way forward for development. On the contrary, I would argue that it is vital to keep sight of the agenda amidst the fog of uncertainties.

Women's human rights, as laid down in international and domestic law, are best seen as a set of political and legal tools. Like other tools, they can be misused. They may not suit every job that needs doing, some need sharpening, and perhaps we need to invent some new ones too as we notice new problems that need fixing. Their effectiveness depends on how skilfully campaigners and activists use them. In the end, the test of their worth is whether or not they help ordinary women in their struggles against discrimination and inequality. The hundreds of women whose work is featured in this book can testify to that. From Activa in Chile and Masimanyane Women's Support

Box 2.6: Human rights 'less shiny' than before

'Human rights as a vision and an aspiration has become less shiny, less of a bright highway, owing to the human rights violations in the democracies of the North. As they wage unjust wars, ill-treat prisoners, and break rules, and as the UN is overpowered, the language of human rights does not resonate well in the South.'

Devaki Jain[20]

Centre in South Africa (both featured in this chapter) to Baobab for Women's Human Rights in Nigeria (see Chapter 4), they are all protecting and promoting poor women's human rights in areas such as education, politics and employment. Although they may be invisible in official development rhetoric, they are right at the centre of the development process.

Working with human rights laws in Chile and South Africa

Activa

If only I'd known sooner! This is a completely different way of dealing with life! To be aware of what women have been doing all over the world; and to decide that we're not going to wait any longer for [the authorities] to keep their promises. We're going to put pressure on them to respond now. That's what this is all about!

The words of Rocio, aged 63, reflect how many women felt after taking part in a three-day workshop in Picarquin, Chile, run by women's NGO Activa. Training sessions covered the main international treaties and agreements on women's rights and reducing poverty, notably CEDAW, the Beijing Platform for Action and the Millennium Development Goals, and provided tips on how to monitor local government performance against these commitments.

'Now ... we know about Beijing, discrimination and the rights we have; until now, we'd never discussed such international summits and how they can help us here,' said Teresa, another participant.

The workshop also looked at the history of local and international women's movements, so that participants could learn about women's struggles and achievements in the past.[21]

Masimanyane Women's Support Centre

Masimanyane is a South African NGO working on domestic violence and sexual abuse in the Eastern Cape. Their experience with CEDAW is a model of how other women's organisations can use the treaty. One of their most successful advocacy strategies was the development of a CEDAW shadow report, which was submitted to the UN CEDAW Committee in 1998. The report provided an extensive analysis on violence against women in South Africa, pointing out the weaknesses in the way government and civil society were addressing the issue. After Masimanyane presented this, the Committee used it to make several recommendations to the South African government. Its recommendations on equality and non-discrimination against women led to the development of equality legislation, which was passed in 2000.

This shows how grassroots women's experiences can be taken up by the international community and lead to national action. According to Lesley Anne Foster, Masimanyane's Director, CEDAW is 'an instrument that changes women's lives concretely'.[21] Inspired by Masimanyane's own success in using CEDAW, she is Head of the Africa Section of the Global CEDAW Optional Protocol Campaign, and trains activists in the region on how best to lobby their governments to adopt it.

3
The threat of cultural relativism

Universalism – the idea that human rights apply to everyone – is one of the most important principles of the human rights tradition. Can we respect cultural diversity without violating it? Feminists living in conservative societies in the global South think human rights apply to them just as to other women, but their opponents argue that rights are contingent on the customs, practices and values of the cultures that women inhabit.

> Human rights are the right to be the same and the right to be different.
>
> Justice Albie Sachs of the Constitutional Court of South Africa[1]

One of the most important principles underlying human rights is that they apply to everyone; in other words they are universal. However, opponents of human rights in the global South often argue that they are based on a specifically Western political tradition, and so are not appropriate to other societies, a position called 'cultural relativism'. Some see human rights as a form of imperialism imposed by the rich countries of the global North on other cultures. In the 1990s, for instance, the East Asian leaders Lee Kuan Yew in Singapore and Mahathir Mohamad in Malaysia claimed that human rights were not suited to Asian societies, which prioritised social order and stability over individual freedom. However, there are plenty of Asian dissidents and activists who are struggling for human rights, one of the best-known being Aung San Suu Kyi in Burma. That suggests cultural relativism is really a political position, rather than a cultural one.[2]

How cultural relativism threatens women

Cultural relativism is an especially dangerous idea when it comes to *women's* human rights. Many cultures have traditionally exercised strict control over girls and women, reflected in a wide range of customs and practices, such as female genital mutilation (FGM), the removal of part or all of the female genitalia. Routine domestic violence and the exclusion of women from inheriting land are also examples of cultural practices that harm women's human rights in one way or another. Perhaps this is why self-appointed guardians of cultures are often preoccupied with women's status and behaviour. In particular, societies or groups that somehow feel threatened, for instance immigrant communities, often seem to put forward women as symbols of their cultural distinctiveness. A few years ago I spent some time in the Tibetan refugee community of Mundgod, in the Indian state of Karnataka. Most older women in the settlement wore the traditional Tibetan outfit of a long, dark wraparound dress and striped apron, but I only once saw a man wearing the male version of Tibetan traditional dress. On the contrary, most men in the community, including the older generation, seemed to prefer a more modern, sophisticated image, dressing in Western style with shirts and trousers.[3]

This identification of women with traditional culture can be relatively benign, as seems to be the case with the Mundgod example, or it can be used for sinister purposes. This is what seems to have happened in the Pakistani Muslim community in Bradford, in the United Kingdom, in the late 1990s, when gangs of young Muslim men took it upon themselves to police young Muslim women's clothes and behaviour. Women who went out in the evening, or wore clothes that the gangs judged 'inappropriate', were harassed, threatened, and in some cases attacked. According to Maree Stacey, who worked with women in this community, the gang members themselves had Western life-styles, but were manipulating an idea of Pakistani Muslim culture in order to promote their own power and interests.[4]

One of the reasons cultural relativism poses such a threat for women's human rights is that, to outsiders at least, it can seem reasonable. According to academic Deniz Kandiyoti, 'We need to accept the possibility of difference, difference in conceptions of ... the good life.'[5] Surely human rights have to take cultural diversity into account, as this and Judge Albie Sachs' comment at the start of this chapter suggest? The question is, who decides which human rights are appropriate for women in a given society and which are not. It is usually dominant groups, mostly men, who define 'their' cultures. This may entail a call to tradition, but not all traditions are worth being preserved; see Box 3.1, for instance, on the consequences of girls' early marriage in Nigeria.

Cultures are always changing

Does anyone today bemoan the end of foot-binding in China, unique cultural tradition though it was? Reflecting on my own culture, I am often struck by how much attitudes regarding women's status have changed since I was a child. I sometimes remember a visit from an aunt and uncle when I was about eight; hearing I was doing well at school, they shook their heads because it was me rather than my brother getting top marks: 'It's a waste when it's the girls. After all, they don't need to be brainy, do they?' Going even further back, there used to be an English proverb: 'A woman, a dog and a walnut tree, the more you beat them, the better they be.' Thankfully it is rarely heard now except occasionally as a 'joke', showing how English culture, specifically attitudes towards domestic violence, has evolved since it was current. This is not to say

Box 3.1: Girls' Early Marriage in Nigeria[6]

Among the Ibibios of eastern Nigeria, girls can be married off as young as 13, and poor, uneducated girls usually marry in their early teens. The tradition survives because women have few options except marriage and mother-hood, and there are various pressures on girls' parents to conform with it. They may want to please village elders, get the 'bride price' paid by the husband's family, or create alliances between families. They often worry that their daughters might get pregnant while still unmarried, disgracing themselves and their families.

But early marriage carries serious consequences for both individual girls and society in general. Most girls who marry early are expected to work in the husband's household, so they have to drop out of school. Their lack of education then limits their ability to care for their children, contribut-ing to high infant mortality and illness and perpetuating the cycle of ignorance and disadvantage. Then there are the health risks associated with early pregnancy. A recent survey found that, in the north-west of Nigeria, 55 per cent of girls aged between 15–19 were either mothers or preg-nant. When girls give birth before they are physically mature, they often have to endure prolonged labour, jeop-ardising both baby and mother. Only a very small propor-tion of Nigerians have access to health care, so girls are very unlikely to get medical help during their labour, even if there are complications.[7] The result is that Nigeria has one of the highest maternal mortality rates in the world: 1,500 deaths for every 100,000 births.

Vesico-vaginal fistulae or VVF is a condition arising from early marriage and pregnancy. VVF is an abnormal, tube-like passage that opens up between the uterus and bladder or rectum, and can be caused by obstructed childbirth. It causes chronic incontinence, and is one of the most appalling misfortunes a Nigerian woman can face, often leading to humiliation, abandonment by her husband and social ostracism. There are an estimated 150,000 cases of VVF in Nigeria, although it has been more or less wiped out in the developed world. The only cure is reconstructive surgery, which is way beyond the reach of most Nigerian women.

Early marriage contravenes the Convention on the Rights of the Child, which the Nigerian Federal Government has signed. The government recently enacted legislation to bring it into line with the Convention, but researcher Eno-Obong Akpan thinks that this will not be enough to end early marriage. She says only a combination of social and economic factors, including improved education, job opportunities for women and higher incomes, can make a significant impact on this aspect of Nigerian culture.

that domestic violence is a thing of the past in the UK, only that mainstream culture no longer condones it.

The point I am trying to make is that customs and traditions are not sacrosanct, and cultures, whether we like it or not, are changing all the time as people develop and adapt new ideas, some from within their own societies and some from outside. Economic globalisation is a major factor in this, bringing about enormous cultural change in places like Bangladesh, where 1.8 million jobs for women have been created in the garment industry, drawing them into paid work for the first time (Box 3.2). This is challenging the tradition of purdah, whereby women stay at home and keep out of public life. We all know that our own cultures are changing, so we should not expect other people's to stay frozen in time.

Box 3.2: Globalisation and change in Bangladesh

During the 1990s, when firms in the global North began to out-source garment manufacturing to low-income countries, large numbers of clothing factories started to open up in Dhaka, the capital of Bangladesh. An estimated 1.8 million jobs were created, 90 per cent of them for women. Young women from rural areas were seen as ideal workers for these new enterprises, which exported to Europe and the United States. The 'pull' of the new job opportunities coincided with 'push' factors that were driving young women into the city. Increasing poverty and changes in social relations in Bangladesh's rural areas meant that many young women there found themselves devoid of support and with no means of making a decent living. Thousands flocked to Dhaka to take up the new jobs, and commentators marvelled at the sight of them as they walked from their homes in the slums to the factories every morning; Bangladesh had seen nothing like it before. Women going to work on their own challenged the tradition of seclusion or purdah, whereby women stay in the home and do not venture into the public world.

In 2004, BBC journalist Roland Buerk talked to Ayesha Khatun, one of the women who moved to Dhaka to work in a garment factory. She had a job trimming loose threads on finished clothes, and did not regret the move, telling him: 'In the villages there are no jobs. In Dhaka there are opportunities. We can get a job, then we can live, eat; we can do everything in Dhaka. Dhaka is better.' She was earning $50 a month, which she considered to be good money.[8]

'These women emerged as the first generation of women workers in this country,' said Mashuda Khatun

Shefali, of the Centre for Women's Initiatives, an organisation offering classes in job-hunting for unemployed garment workers. 'Once these women were earning money, they achieved some decision-making capacity in their families and in their personal lives.'

There are predictions that thousands of Bangladesh's women workers will lose their jobs in the face of increased competition from India and China. If that happens, will they return to their villages and live as before? Or will they stay in the cities, with their hard-won freedoms?

Cultural relativism is simplistic. It fails to acknowledge that cultures are permeated by power relations, and that they are dynamic, sophisticated and constantly interacting with one another. If we take cultural relativism to its logical conclusion, we have to accept any behaviour, however cruel or degrading, provided it is condoned by the culture it happens in. Still, it is a highly effective weapon for attacking women's human rights, as feminists in the global South know only too well. By labelling women's human rights as a post-colonialist imposition, their enemies have tried to isolate and undermine them; see Maitrayee Mukhopadhyay's remark in Box 3.3. At the same time, many feminists and rights activists in the global North are afraid to criticise other cultures for fear of being branded racist. Development aid agencies, too, tend to be sensitive to accusations of cultural imperialism. While this is understandable, they should not be intimidated into uncritically accepting cultural practices that harm women's human rights.

All over the global South, home-grown women's organisations are tackling values and practices that harm women, through activities that reflect, as well as challenge, their own cultures. The development of an alternative 'rite of passage' for Kenyan girls who would otherwise undergo FGM is a

Box 3.3: Feminists in the global South: 'Westernised'?

'In my work in India, I was operating in my own society and culture, and so was speaking as an "insider". Despite this, it was in my work for gender equity that I most often experienced allegations from different quarters that this work was against our culture, violated our traditions, and the worst criticism of all in the Indian context, that it was "Westernised".'[9]

Maitrayee Mukhopadhyay

fascinating example of this kind of creativity; see below. This case study also shows how, as cultural 'outsiders', development aid agencies (in this case PATH, a US-based NGO) can nevertheless play a useful role by funding and supporting the work of progressive 'insiders'. It highlights an interesting point; the line between cultural sensitivity and cultural relativism may, at times, be very thin.

Circumcision with words

Female genital mutilation (FGM) is the partial or total removal of girls' external genitalia. There are different forms of FGM, some more severe than others. It occurs primarily in over 25 African countries, among some minorities in Asia and in some immigrant communities in Europe, Australia, Canada and the United States. Every year, an estimated 2 million girls undergo FGM. In African communities where it is practised, FGM is often performed as part of a coming-of-age ritual, marking girls' transition to womanhood. Uncircumcised women are seen as undesirable, a threat to the social order, so there is a social pressure on girls' mothers and other female relatives to get girls circumcised.

The practice violates women's sexual rights and can cause serious health complications, threatening their very right to life. In the short term, FGM is painful and often frightening, and there is a risk of contracting infections; most FGM procedures are carried out without anaesthetic, using rudimentary instruments in unsanitary conditions. In the longer term, women who have undergone FGM may suffer lifelong complications, and they are twice as likely to die during childbirth.

FGM is widespread in Kenya despite the Children's Act of 2001 which prohibits forced FGM. Kenya has also signed the women's rights supplementary protocol to the African Charter on Human and Peoples' Rights, which requires signatory governments to prohibit the practice. Since the mid 1990s, the Kenyan women's umbrella organisation Maendeleo Ya Wanawake (MYWO), supported by international NGO PATH, has been using alternative rites of passage to combat FGM. These are modified ceremonies that retain most of the features of traditional coming-of-age ceremonies, namely seclusion, family life education, celebration and gift-giving, but without any physical harm being done to girls. The first such ceremony took place in 1996, in a village near Mount Kenya. Since then there have been many more, and by 1998 an estimated 1,100 girls had gone through this 'circumcision with words', as it is known. Public participation has been strong, involving village elders, parents, religious leaders and boys, who are asked to make a pact to support their sisters.

Although FGM is a deep-rooted cultural tradition, modified rites, supported by good communications and public awareness raising, offer an acceptable compromise for many – although not all – people in the communities concerned. The approach has two obvious strengths. First, it is led by local people themselves; much of the original impetus came from mothers looking for ways to save their daughters from the painful and dangerous operation. Second, it accommodates local culture as far as possible, rather than flouting it. However, women's rights activist Saida Ali, who has worked on a programme combating FGM in north-east Kenya's refugee camps, points out that the approach does not address the issue of women's sexual rights or challenge conservative ideas of how women should behave. Many circumcised women find it hard to achieve sexual satisfaction, and she says FGM is really about controlling women's sexuality. Women's sexuality rights were established at the International Conference on Population and Development in Cairo and the Fourth World Conference on Women in Beijing in the mid-1990s. They include women's right 'to have control over and decide freely and responsibly on matters related to their sexuality, including sexual and reproductive health, free of coercion, discrimination and violence'.[10] Ms Ali told Kathambi Kinoti of the Association for Women's Rights in Development:

> Ideally, FGM eradication programmes should address the sexuality rights of every girl and woman. We cannot ignore the cultural mindset of communities that practise FGM and this has tended to take priority over the assertion of sexuality rights. However, it is possible by concerted efforts to replace the community and its slanted values with the individual woman and her personhood, with her attendant inherent human rights.[11]

'Circumcision with words' raises interesting questions for development workers and women's rights activists working in socially conservative communities. A rights-based approach would set out to change people's beliefs and views about women's sexuality and how they should behave, but in many contexts that can be counter-productive. Many would argue that compromises are acceptable if that is the only way to protect girls from harmful practices like FGM. Nevertheless, Ms Ali's question is thought-provoking: 'It is all well and good to take into account the culture of the community, but does cultural relativism supersede the inherent sexuality rights of women?'[12]

4
'Not a fax from heaven'

The political manipulation of religious teachings, in the form of so-called 'fundamentalist' versions of different faiths, has put women's rights advocates on the defensive all over the world. They have responded with a range of strategies. Some take a purely secular position, while others are working within religious discourses to oppose conservative forces, showing that texts such as the Bible and Qur'an can be interpreted as supporting women's human rights.

> Fundamentalism is growing in many world religions today and is damaging women's rights in all of them.
> Women against Fundamentalisms[1]

Since 9/11, the Madrid bombings of 2004 and the London bombings of 2005, the words 'Islamic' and 'fundamentalist' have frequently been coupled together in headlines in the global North. They have created a stereotype that many Muslims find insulting and alarming. The common, but sloppy, identification of religious fundamentalism with Islam is racist. It has set up the idea that all Muslims are fundamentalist, and overlooks the fact that other faiths, not least Christianity, have their own forms of fundamentalism too.[2] In reality, religious fundamentalisms are conservative political forces that use religious texts such as the Bible or the Qur'an in their struggles for power and social control.[3] Another common factor is that they are all preoccupied with controlling women. In the fundamentalist mindset, women exist mainly as wives and mothers, and represent 'authentic' values.

The proponents of fundamentalism work at all levels from

international policy-making arenas to the streets. Starting with the International Conference on Population and Development in Cairo in 1994, representatives of Islamic and Christian fundamentalist movements united at successive UN events to oppose progress on women's sexual and reproductive rights. And in communities where grassroots fundamentalist groups are strong, ordinary women's very right to life can be at stake if they are seen to transgress the rules laid down for them (Box 4.1). This chapter briefly looks at the impact of Christian and Islamic fundamentalisms on women's human rights, but it is important to remember that other faiths, notably Hinduism and Judaism, have fundamentalist sections too.

Box 4.1: Death by vigilantes

Photographs of 19-year-old Yousra al-Azam show a round-faced, confident-looking young woman, her hair entirely covered by a black scarf. One day in April 2005, she went shopping with her fiancé in Gaza City. She was looking for a wedding dress. Later, together with Yousra's sister and her fiancé, they went to the beach. On their way back home that evening, a vehicle full of masked and armed men forced their car to pull over. Yousra was shot dead; her sister was beaten with clubs. The attackers were members of Hamas. Calling themselves 'morality police', they threatened to shoot passers-by who tried to stop the attack. According to the BBC, 'it seems that – in the eyes of the gunmen – something in the behaviour of the couples had been deemed unacceptable in Islamic terms.'

Hamas leaders were quick to disassociate themselves from the murder: 'It was an irresponsible act, and it was against the policy of Hamas.' However, critics suggested that giving young men guns, and preaching an extreme notion of Islamic morality, might have led to the killing.[4]

Fundamentalisms and resistance

Let us begin with the Catholic Church hierarchy. Although describing it as a fundamentalist body might come as a surprise, that is the view of the campaign group Women Against Fundamentalisms (WAF), which points out that fundamentalists occupy positions of authority and power as well as existing on the margins.[5] When he was still Cardinal Joseph Ratzinger, Pope Benedict XVI was known in some quarters as 'God's Rottweiler' and, like his predecessor Pope John Paul II, he is firmly opposed to all forms of artificial contraception. Millions of Roman Catholics across the world disagree with and ignore this policy (see Box 4.2, for instance). Forcing women to rely only on natural forms of contraception in effect means taking away their right to choose how many children to have, and how to space them. If women cannot control this aspect of their lives, their health is put at risk, it becomes all the harder for them to exercise their rights in other areas, such as education or employment, and poverty for them and their children is perpetuated. Yet, back in 1994, the Vatican allied with the Islamic fundamentalist government of Iran to try to prevent a progressive agreement on women's reproductive rights, and as I write this, the Roman Catholic Church in Guatemala is planning legal challenges to new legislation requiring the government to promote contraception. This in a country where 50 per cent of women have had a child by the age of 19, and infant mortality and malnutrition are among the highest in the region.[6]

The Vatican's opposition to condoms is also weakening the fight against HIV/AIDS in Africa, where the UN estimates that 80 million Africans may die from the disease by 2025. Shortly after taking office in 2005, the new Pope told African bishops that the epidemic had to be tackled through fidelity and abstinence, not condoms, and warned that 'a contraception mentality' was threatening the fabric of African life.[7] Prior to this, 2003 saw a major row between the Vatican and the World Health

Organization, after senior Vatican officials spread the disinformation that condoms were ineffective against HIV infection.[8] The debate on the use of condoms in the context of the HIV/AIDS epidemic is by no means closed though, even within the Catholic Church's highest ranks. At the time of writing, a liberal cardinal has publicly challenged the Pope's view, telling an Italian magazine that in couples where one partner has HIV/AIDS, the use of condoms is 'a lesser evil' than the other partner becoming infected.[9]

Meanwhile, Protestant Christian fundamentalists in the United States wield such strong influence over President Bush that they have, in effect, taken control of US aid policies on reproductive rights, affecting millions of women in low-income countries (Box 4.3).

As for Islamic fundamentalism, a debate is raging in Muslim communities all over the world on the relationship between

Box 4.2: Catholics for a Free Choice

Catholics for a Free Choice (CFFC), which originated in the United States but also has branches throughout Latin America, has for many years opposed the Vatican's stance on contraception. CFFC points out that:

> contrary to the conventional wisdom, the morality of artificial contraception is by no means a closed subject within the Catholic Church. It is a matter of continuing and lively discussion within the hierarchy, among theologians and by lay Catholics. The encyclical 'Humanae Vitae', which proscribes the use of artificial contraception by Catholics, was described by the Vatican as 'not infallible' teaching. While Catholics need to take this teaching quite seriously, there is room for legitimate dissent.[10]

Box 4.3: The global gag rule

On his first day in the White House in 2001, George W. Bush reinstated the 'global gag rule', a policy first imposed by President Reagan in 1984 and then overturned by President Clinton. This bars NGOs from receiving US funds if they use other, non-US, funds to perform abortions, provide abortion counselling or lobby for more lenient abortion laws. An earlier rule already prohibited the direct use of US aid for abortion.

The gag rule forced family-planning and reproductive-health organisations to make a hard choice. Either they accepted US cash, along with its accompanying constraints, or rejected what was for many their biggest source of funding. According to Population Action, the gag rule has caused clinics in Kenya, Ghana and Bangladesh to close. The Family Planning Association of Kenya refused to accept it on principle, even though it neither performs abortions nor offers abortion counselling. The International Planned Parenthood Federation lost $12 million in aid, plus a further $75 million that it expected for programmes run jointly with other agencies. Worldwide, thousands of low-income women have been deprived of their only access to family-planning services and pre and post-natal care.

The destructive attentions of the US Christian right have now turned to HIV prevention programmes that target sex workers. For instance, Population Services International (PSI) saw funding for its HIV prevention programme in Central America cut off after Republican Senator Tom Coburn complained about it to President Bush. The Senator objected to PSI workers demonstrating how to use condoms in bars frequented by sex workers. According to

> Rev. Tim Simpson of the Christian Alliance, 'This is an absolutely tragic situation that is being compounded by the extremist ethics of Christian fundamentalists who place sexual purity ahead of saving lives.'[11]

Islamic principles and women's human rights. Conservative Muslims reject universalism and argue instead that men and women have different, complementary rights, based on their distinct social roles. For instance, when Iraqi feminists protested against references to Sharia in parts of the country's new constitution in August 2005, there were other women counter-protesting, shouting slogans objecting to 'absolute equality'.[12] In practice, so-called 'complementarity' between men's and women's rights often masks discrimination against women, for instance in inheritance matters. In general, the Islamic law on inheritance gives female relatives smaller shares of property than males, and women a weaker claim than men's, on the grounds that men are responsible for supporting women in the family.

Many conservative Muslims argue that women's subordination is divinely ordained, because it is codified in Sharia. But Sharia is a product of centuries of human (mostly male) interpretation of Islamic religious laws, and there is great diversity between religious laws in different parts of the Muslim world. Although many people in the United States and Europe think of Islam as an Arab religion, in fact millions of Muslims live in south and south-east Asia, sub-Saharan Africa and south-east Europe. As Fatou Sow points out in Box 4.4, there is no such thing as 'the Muslim woman'.

The diversity of Islamic religious law suggests that it is not Islam itself that is a barrier to women achieving their human rights in these countries, but its misuse. On the other hand, many

Box 4.4: The diversity of Muslim women

There is not one type of Muslim woman; they differ according to their countries, culture, language and other influences; the Sharia laws are interpreted differently within these influences and resolve issues in different ways. The Muslim world is not one world, but exists in different places.

Fatou Sow, Development Alternatives
with Women for a New Era (DAWN)[13]

Muslim scholars, lawyers and activists all over the world have developed interpretations of the Qur'an that support women's human rights, such as Siti Musdah Mullia in Indonesia (see Box 4.5). When conservative, often undemocratic governments need to appease fundamentalist groups, women's rights become a pawn in the political game. Women's rights have been traded in this way by both powerful men and women.

Impact of the 'war on terror'

Fundamentalist religious movements are often explained as an extreme reaction to the fragmentation and confusion of the modern world, and they can appeal to both women and men. The so-called war on terror has inflamed fundamentalist tendencies in some regions. I talked to Cassandra Balchin, who works with Women Living Under Muslim Laws (WLUML), about the implications for women's human rights (Box 4.6).

Despite fundamentalism's appeal to some women, as well as men, many men and women are nonetheless resisting such movements. Some operate inside their faith, like Siti Musdah Mulia. Others take a purely secular position, arguing that human rights take precedence over religious teaching. In

Box 4.5: Siti Musdah Mulia, a tool for Western concepts?[14]

Siti Musdah Mulia has attracted fierce hostility for criticising aspects of Islam that some people consider sacred. Although she herself wears the traditional head covering, for example, she says this is an entirely personal decision that is not mandated by any religious directive.

Perhaps her opponents are particularly disconcerted because she is highly qualified to speak on the subject: she studied Islamic political thinking at Syahid Institute of Islamic Studies in Jakarta, where she was the top doctoral graduate, and was the first woman to gain a PhD in the field. She is a champion of gender equality and strives to shift religious thinking towards it. The conservatives, she comments, 'used to annoy me, but now I pity them. I think their narrow-mindedness is due to limited access to knowledge and the opportunity to see the other side.'

But the accusation that she is a tool of Westernisation hurts. 'That makes me feel so sad. I don't need people to pay me to fight for humanity, to formulate Islamic teachings that are more friendly to women. ... People always say that religious teachings are final, it's God's law, no need to tinker with them. That statement especially arises during the discussion of marital law. I tell them that the whole marital law is manmade, none of it is a fax from heaven. ... The concept of equality, fraternity and equality must not be claimed as Western ... and Muslims must not think of it as Western related. It's a universal value.'

Nigeria, Baobab for Women's Human Rights is mixing both secular and faith-based strategies to counter the recent introduction of extremely conservative legislation, allegedly based on Sharia, in the country's northern states.

Box 4.6: Interview with Cassandra Balchin

G.T. The so-called 'war on terror' led by the US, with the UK as its most important ally, has already caused a backlash that threatens women's human rights in some regions. Do you think this trend will continue?

C.B. Yes; for various reasons, not least continuing global economic inequalities and the USA's overwhelming dominance in the current world order, it seems that in the near future fundamentalisms based on ethnic, cultural or religious identities will get stronger. Dominant forces such as the US government, as well as opposition political groups, are misusing religion for political gain. We can see an immediate impact of the 'war on terror' in Iran. Suddenly, after a period of growing liberalisation, demanding democracy and criticising the Iranian government was once again seen as synonymous with being 'pro-US'. In recent elections in both Pakistan and Iran, highly conservative governments were elected, and analysts see this as a direct backlash against the 'war on terror'. Women have already begun to experience an impact on their rights to mobility and freedom from violence, in public and at home. In Iran, the conservative swing at the end of 2004 saw leading women's activist Mahboobeh Abbasgholizadeh arrested; she was only released following an international solidarity campaign. The government clamped down on the country's vibrant blogging scene and bloggers, including many young women who had used blogging to push the boundaries of discussion on women's roles, were hounded.

G.T. How should progressives in the global North, particularly feminists, respond?

C.B. It is over ten years since the Beijing Fourth World Conference on Women. Women's rights activists all over the world are reassessing their strategies for strengthening women's rights and challenging poverty. Central to this is a rethinking on culture and religion. There is now a 'politically correct' assumption that religion (and not class, age, ethnicity, disability, orientation and so on) is the most important developmental issue for women in the South, especially in Muslim contexts. In extreme cases, people in progressive and left circles in Europe and North America have even entered into alliances with so-called 'moderate Islamists', especially in opposition to the war in Iraq. The British political party 'Respect', for instance, is an alliance of left-wing parliamentarians and anti-war activists with the Muslim Council of Britain. Muslim women's groups were outraged when they discovered that a charity listed on the Council's website as one of its affiliates was promoting female genital mutilation (FGM). The reference to FGM was removed after a report to the Charities Commission. Women in Muslim contexts who have directly experienced the impact of fundamentalisms on their daily lives are urging their friends in the developed world to understand that unholy alliances like this one mean giving prominence to religious leaders. Although these 'moderates' may give lip-service to women's rights, their vision of society and development is profoundly inequitable.

Baobab for Women's Human Rights

The Nigerian organisation Baobab for Women's Human Rights is best known for defending women's rights under Muslim laws, in particular the Sharia criminal legislation passed in several northern Nigerian states since 2000. The new legislation arose from political power struggles in the region. In effect, it panders to the Muslim religious right, but according to Baobab the way it has been used is a travesty of even conservative Islamic jurisprudence. For instance, more women than men have been accused of adultery, with its penalty of stoning to death, while a woman making a charge of rape has to produce four male witnesses of 'impeccable character', a grotesquely unfair requirement. In Zamfara state, gangs of local vigilantes, mostly unemployed young men, used the expansion of Sharia to 'police' women's clothes, and women were banned from sitting with men on buses and in taxis. There is no basis for either of these restrictions in Islamic jurisprudence.

Baobab was the first NGO with members from the Muslim community to speak out against what its coordinator Ayesha Imam is careful to call the 'abuse of Sharia' in northern Nigeria. Since then, its staff and volunteers have worked constantly to open up the new laws to discussion, refusing to be intimidated. As well as a national office in Lagos, Baobab has volunteer outreach teams working in 14 Nigerian states. They raise awareness of women's rights issues through theatre, radio jingles and debates, run paralegal training courses for NGOs and provide mediation and counselling.

One of Baobab's first reactions to the expansion of Sharia was to hold a series of 'bridge-building' workshops, involving Muslims from all walks of life. Scholars, rights activists, conservatives and progressives from all over the country came together for several days to examine Qur'anic teachings on issues affecting women, such as divorce, and discuss interpretations. They looked at the potential for Muslim laws to support women's rights, as well as critiquing negative interpretations. Since then there have been several such workshops, including one for the whole West Africa region that showed how Muslim laws vary from one community to another.

Most of the public attention Baobab gets is for its work defending victims of Sharia. Although many are women, Baobab also defends men and boys, for instance minors sentenced to amputation for theft. The organisation also defends women's rights against abuses under statutory and customary law. In 2002, one of the cases Baobab was involved in led to international headlines and a global letter-writing campaign. A Sharia court in Katsina State sentenced Amina Lawal to death by stoning after she confessed to having had a child while divorced. Charges against the man concerned were dropped, after he reportedly denied having sex with her.

The international letter-writing campaign was based on the false information that Ms Lawal's appeal had failed, whereas in fact she had yet to begin the appeal process. In a press release, Ayesha Imam called for a halt to the letters, setting out the reasons Baobab wanted them to stop. First, she pointed out that they could well backfire. Baobab had every reason to be concerned about this, because of an earlier experience. In 2001, the Governor of Zamfara State reacted to another misguided letter campaign by bringing forward the flogging of Bariya Magazu, a 13-year-old girl found guilty of extra-marital sex, thus pre-empting her legal appeal. Baobab staff were convinced they would have won the appeal, as she was legally too young to be convicted. Ms Imam also argued that, in situations like Amina Lawal's, pursuing cases through the courts is a much better strategy. Successful legal challenges make it clear that such convictions and sentences are wrong, whereas 'a pardon means that people are guilty but the state is forgiving them'. She asked the letter-writers to respect local activists' skills and knowledge and let them handle the situation themselves. Six months after the stoning sentence, Amina Lawal's conviction was quashed by the Katsina court of appeal.

Some of the campaigning letters from the United States and Europe were very hostile to Islam in general, showing the prevalence of negative stereotypes in the global North. In fact, members of Amina Lawal's community had themselves criticised her conviction and protected her from Islamist vigilantes, and in general she had strong public support in Nigeria, and also from the media, women lawyers, and women's groups from the North. Baobab has received help for its work against retrogressive laws from lawyers, rights activists and progressive Islamic scholars from all over the Muslim world. As Ayesha Imam is careful to point out: 'We are not anti-Islam, we are pro-just Muslim laws'.

5
The podium and the polling booth

By rights, about 50 per cent of the world's MPs should be women, but the actual proportion is only 17 per cent. Women's rights to stand for and hold office, vote, lobby and campaign for change are closely linked to all their other rights; if women do not engage in politics, our issues remain invisible. Strategies for increasing women's participation in political life range from small-scale empowerment to national quota systems. Even after taking up office, women often need support to operate independently from male-dominated power structures.

> We are part of the composition of this society, we have to be part of the present and the future of this country, so we have to also participate in the making of this modern country, we cannot leave it only to the men to decide for us. We are human beings; we are half of this society, we are half of the population, and it is our right to have a say.
>
> Amal Basha, Sisters' Arabic Forum, Yemen

As Amal Basha so cogently argues, it is a matter of simple justice that women, who number roughly half the population, should also number half of the world's political representatives. Yet, as we all know, the actual state of affairs is very different. Women hold only 17 per cent of parliamentary seats worldwide, ranging from 41 per cent in Nordic countries to 8 per cent in Arab States.[1] There is no automatic correlation between national affluence and women's share of parliamentary seats; Rwanda, Cuba, Costa Rica and Mozambique are all in the 'top ten' nations, higher than the United States, the UK and most developed countries (see Table 5.1).

Why is women's political participation important?

Women's right to stand for and hold political office, on bodies ranging from international commissions to village councils, is a crucial aspect of our political rights. Other rights in this area are the right to vote and the right to take part in political and public life, for instance by belonging to an NGO or informal association. The rights to vote and stand for office are concerned with direct involvement in politics, while the right to lobby and campaign are about influencing public policies and how they are implemented. Put simply, political rights are about taking part in making the decisions that affect all our lives – and on an equal basis with men.

As far as international human rights legislation is concerned, women's political rights are covered in Article 7 of CEDAW. But citing a dry legal text does not give due credit to the women who, for decades, have struggled to win these formal rights – in particular the right to vote. In the UK, for instance, the women's suffrage movement of the early part of the twentieth century is the most famous feminist struggle in our history. Today, the same struggle continues in Saudi Arabia, where women were not allowed to vote or stand for office in 2005's municipal elections. The government has promised they will be able to vote in the next elections, scheduled for 2009. Many of the rights covered in this book, including political rights, are linked to others, because not being able to exercise one right can undermine other rights too. Women's marginalisation from power, which is overwhelmingly in men's hands, means that international, national and local priorities are defined with little contribution from

Table 5.1 Proportion of women in national parliaments (top ten nations)

Rank	Country	Lower house/single house				Upper house/Senate			
		Elections	Seats No.	women	% women	Elections	Seats No.	women	% women
1	Rwanda	09 2003	80	39	48.8	09 2003	26	9	34.6
2	Sweden	09 2002	349	158	45.3	–	–	–	–
3	Norway	09 2005	169	64	37.9	–	–	–	–
4	Finland	03 2003	200	75	37.5	–	–	–	–
5	Denmark	02 2005	179	66	36.9	–	–	–	–
6	Netherlands	01 2003	150	55	36.7	06 2003	75	22	29.3
7	Cuba	01 2003	609	219	36.0	–	–	–	–
"	Spain	03 2004	350	126	36.0	03 2004	259	60	23.2
8	Costa Rica	02 2006	57	20	35.1	–	–	–	–
9	Argentina	10 2005	257	90	35.0	10 2005	72	30	41.7
10	Mozambique	12 2004	250	87	34.8	–	–	–	–

Data from Inter-Parliamentary Union, updated on 28 February 2006 <www.ipu.org>.

women, and this makes it harder to change government policies and actions that undermine women's other rights. These include official failure to punish violence against women, inadequate childcare provision, unequal pay, schools that do not meet girls' needs, and many other types of discrimination. Given the gross gender imbalance in political representation, it is not surprising that in many countries legislation, legal systems and government policies fail to reflect, or worse, actively discriminate against, women's particular needs and interests. On the other hand, the achievements of Doris Solis Carrion in Ecuador illustrate, on a small scale, what women can do for women's human rights once they gain office (Box 5.1).

Of course, having women in high office is not invariably good news for women's rights. Margaret Thatcher's long period as Prime Minister of Great Britain between 1979 and 1990 demonstrated that point very convincingly. In fact, part of her recipe for success in a man's world was precisely that she distanced herself from women's issues. She also kept other women out of her government, at least as far as senior positions were concerned. So there is no automatic relationship between the gender of individual power holders and the policies they pursue, and we

Box 5.1: Achievements of a woman mayor in Ecuador

After becoming the first female vice Mayor of Cuenca in Ecuador, Doris Solis Carrion spearheaded an equal opportunities plan, including improved services for domestic violence victims. For six years she worked tirelessly on the issue, helped by a quota law that ushered large numbers of Ecuadorian women into political posts and so moved it up the public agenda. As a result of her work, Cuenca now has a hotline, counselling projects and a shelter for abused women.[2]

cannot assume that any particular woman in power will stand up for women's rights. Rather, in the words of the Executive Director of the UN Development Fund for Women (UNIFEM), putting more women in power would help to create a level playing field (Box 5.2). The BPFA recommended that governments set a target of 30 per cent of seats for women in national parliaments; evidence suggests that before women can have any real influence on political processes they need to hold at least this proportion. It is a target that only 15 countries have met, several of which are in the global South. Many of these are newly democratic countries which have taken the opportunity to set up structures promoting women's political participation.

Political participation and poverty

What about poor women in the global South? At first sight, being able to take part in politics, in whatever way, might seem like an irrelevance, or even a luxury, as far as they are concerned. After all, many have their work cut out just coping with the grinding deprivation they face every day. This leads to the question: What is the relationship between political rights and poverty? Oxfam, whose core mission is to wipe out poverty, talks about 'voice poverty', the denial of poor women's and men's right to influence the decisions that affect their lives. For Oxfam, this powerlessness is itself part of the experience of being poor. Ending voice poverty is also a strategy for reducing

Box 5.2: Limitations of women's political representation

'Increasing women's share of seats in parliament is not a panacea. It can only level the playing-field on which women battle for equality.'

UNIFEM[3]

material deprivation, because it means poor women and men can have a say in how resources are used. The trouble is, millions of poor women inhabit a vicious circle. Their daily struggle to survive means they have neither the time nor energy to get involved in even local campaigning that might make a real difference to their well-being. Organisations like OMAFES in Mali have broken this vicious circle by providing a secure economic foundation that women can then move on from to get involved in politics (Box 5.3).

Box 5.3: Women taking part in politics in Mali

When Œuvre malienne d'aide à la Femme et à l'enfant au Sahel (OMAFES), an Oxfam partner organisation, started working with women in a poor district of Bamako, the capital of Mali, they were struggling just to make ends meet. Baba Togola, OMAFES' coordinator, grew up in the district and knew what pressures the women were contending with: 'Women would go to work in the market, but couldn't get credit for their businesses and were illiterate; the wholesalers would cheat them.'

OMAFES ran literacy classes and started a credit scheme, providing the women with a foundation of economic security and helping to build their confidence. Then, in the late 1990s, a new decentralised system of government was introduced. For the first time, people in this district, including women, could elect councillors. With OMAFES support, groups of women met to discuss the new political landscape and how to respond to it. They went as a group to their local councillor and were given a plot of land on which to build an office. They have also lobbied councillors for more schools and clean water. Keita Kendja Souko, one of the women who attends the OMAFES meetings, explained the impact they have had on her: 'In the meetings I realised that changes could be made by women like us, not just people at the top. The training opened our minds.'[4]

What are the barriers?

Saudi Arabia apart, in most countries the problem is not that women lack political rights on paper, but that they cannot exercise them to the same extent as men because of cultural, social and economic barriers. The Fawcett Society, an organisation campaigning for equality between men and women in the UK, cites the 'four Cs' – culture, childcare, cash and confidence – as barriers that prevent women from standing for office. According to the Society, the Welsh Assembly is the only parliament in the world that has an equal number of women and men, thanks to positive discrimination. The 'four Cs' are just as apt when it comes to women in developing countries, but in some societies there are yet other constraints, such as the hostility and even violence of powerful men who think that men alone are entitled to hold office. In many countries, hard-line activists, often linked to fundamentalism, also stand in their way; see the comment in Box 5.4. Box 5.5 looks briefly at women's experience during elections in Afghanistan.

As in Afghanistan, women's inability to vote in parts of Guatemala is also bound up with a general culture of undervaluing women; see Box 5.6.

Quotas and other strategies

Quota systems are a good short-term strategy for increasing women's political representation, but because they reduce the number of political seats available to men, they are often fiercely opposed or manipulated by male politicians. They vary from country to country, partly because they reflect distinct electoral

Box 5.4: An Islamic fundamentalist view

'If we allow women to participate in elections this village will become like Lahore or Karachi or Europe – full of obscenity and vulgarity.'

Maulana Hifz ur-Rehman, a cleric and former jihadi fighter in Frontier Province, Pakistan[5]

Box 5.5: Involving women in Afghanistan's elections

Afghanistan has seen two elections in the last few years. The presidential election in 2004, which ushered Hamid Karzai into power, was intended to draw a line under years of Soviet military occupation, civil war and the tyranny of the Taliban. Conflict and chaos had reduced Afghanistan to one of the poorest countries in the world, with appalling figures for women's health and literacy and, especially during the reign of the Taliban, draconian restrictions on their freedoms. Elections for provincial councils and the lower chamber of parliament followed in September 2005.

The presidential election put down a marker that women's involvement in the political process was to be encouraged and supported. As part of its strategy to make the elections women-friendly, the government hired female election workers, allowed women to have polling cards without photographs, in keeping with cultural norms, and started civic education programmes. This worked to the extent that around 40 per cent of voters in the presidential election were women. In a 2004 survey, the commonest reason women gave for not registering was that they did not have permission, presumably from their husbands or other male relatives, to do so.[6] In the conservative and Taliban-dominated south, women's voting was much lower than the country average; here, fear of attack deterred mobile registration teams from making house calls, the only way to reach many rural women.

The following year saw an improvement as far as voting was concerned, with more women registered to vote than in 2004. In one district where no women at all were registered to vote in 2004, over 15,000 were registered in 2005. Being registered does not necessarily mean women can decide who they vote for, though. Apart from intimidation by local warlords standing for office, which affects both men and women alike, women's rights to vote for the candidate of their choice are also denied in other ways. A woman in the city of Herat put it very succinctly: 'Whoever my husband chooses, I will vote for that person. All my opinions will match those of my husband.'

About 25 per cent of seats in parliament's lower house and on the provincial councils were set aside for women. Although this was a very positive move, female candidates faced severe challenges, and in the event, women accounted for only 12 per cent of parliamentary candidates and 8 per cent of Provincial Council candidates. According to research by Human Rights Watch, security risks were a major worry for would-be female candidates. Both male and female candidates feared the armed factions who sought to control the election and, in the south and east, the Taliban fighters who wanted to disrupt it, but women candidates were worse affected. Many female candidates were independents, without affiliation to any of the contending parties, and so with no protection from any of them. And in general, poor security made it hard for women to travel in rural areas, which limited their campaigning. The Taliban in particular are bitterly hostile to women's involvement in public life, including elections, and there was an escalation of violence in Taliban strongholds just before the election, with several women candidates being killed or injured. Others received death threats or were beaten up. In Zabul, where the Taliban was strongest, so few women were prepared to stand that there were not enough candidates to fill the three seats reserved for women on the Provincial Council.[7] The particularly low proportion of women standing for election to the Provincial Councils reflects the dangers involved in conservative, rural areas, as distinct from Kabul, where MPs mostly operate. A woman candidate told Human Rights Watch: 'Because we are not parliamentary candidates, we don't go to Kabul. We have to stay here with all the commanders in the Provincial Council, so we need security.'[8]

According to the Women's Affairs Minister, Masouda Jalal (herself a candidate in the presidential election the previous year): 'The main reason thousands of women didn't become candidates is that they can't afford the financial expenses.' She claimed that lack of cash to pay for posters, travel and other election expenses was a bigger deterrent to women than poor security.[9] Under the Taliban, women were barred from paid jobs, and even now those women who do work tend to be confined to low-paid work such as teaching. If they are married, their husbands usually control spending. There are other deep-seated handicaps that prevent most women from standing. A mere 14 per cent of girls and women over the age of 15 can read and write, for instance.

Even though it gives women only half of the seats they

should have, the quota system enrages Islamist parties: 'This is eating the rights of men,' said the leader of one, the Party of Islamic Rule.[10] Interviewed for the BBC just before the election, Zarmeena Pathan, a parliamentary candidate from Zabul, saw it very differently: 'For the last 30 years women have had their voice taken from them in this country. We thank God that the new draft constitution gives us some rights, though not enough.'[11]

Box 5.6: Overcoming women's disenfranchisement in Guatemala

Coordination of Indigenous Peasant Community Committees for the Promotion and Education for Peace (COICAPEP) works with women in the Quiche community in Guatemala. In this Mayan group, there is a marked preference for sons rather than daughters – so much so that many fathers have not even bothered to register daughters' births, or have registered them with their own names, which means they show up on official records as male. In one group of 30 women, only five had had their births properly registered.

Depriving these women of citizenship by failing to register them also meant, in effect, that they were disenfranchised. COICAPEP recognised this as part and parcel of their poverty, and decided to tackle this as well as providing more obviously poverty-oriented support such as distributing seeds. According to Isabel Gregoria Garcia Lopez, one of the women concerned:

We didn't know that having identification was important until COICAPEP explained it to us. They said it was important for us to have citizenship. My father didn't register me because I am female. I was registered five years ago. I feel different now because I can fight for my rights as a woman. Before, only men were important in the community meetings.[12]

Since registering she has voted in both local and national elections, and takes a keen interest in politics.

systems, and some work better than others.[13] The experience of post-genocide Rwanda is a very interesting and positive example; see Box 5.7. It may be that, because of Rwanda's unique and painful recent history, quotas were more easily accepted there than in some other national contexts.

Experience shows that, to be really successful, quota systems usually have to be reinforced by other strategies. In Hyderabad, India, for instance, women brought into office through quotas still have problems when it comes to functioning as legitimate political beings; see the story about the work of the Confederation of Voluntary Associations (COVA), at the end of this chapter. So we see yet again the familiar distinction between possessing legal rights and being able to exercise them in a meaningful way. Although the Indian quota system has flaws, COVA demonstrates how women's organisations can capitalise on the political 'spaces' that quota systems open up for women.

'Don't think you've developed horns'

In 1993, a new system of local and municipal councils was set up throughout India, and a third of the seats on these bodies were reserved for women. The quota system had an immediate effect; 350,000 women were elected the following year. Apart from a tiny number of privileged women from powerful political dynasties, such as Indira and Sonia Gandhi, women have traditionally

Box 5.7: Rwanda leads the world on women MPs

In 2003, Rwanda elected a record number of women MPs, moving ahead of Sweden, which had previously had the world's highest proportion. Almost 50 per cent of MPs in Rwanda's lower chamber, and 30 per cent of appointed members in the upper house, are women, transforming the political landscape.

The elections ended a nine-year transition period following the genocide that left an estimated 800,000 ethnic Tutsis and moderate Hutus dead. Oxfam Programme Coordinator Grace Mukagabiro was one of the victims: 'On May 8th 1994 my husband was brutally murdered by armed militias. ... At the same time, his parents, his uncles, his aunts and cousins were also killed. My name was on a list of those to be killed the next day. At midnight I escaped, carrying my three small children and two others whose parents had also died. I was pregnant and my youngest child was 11 months old. We walked 18 kilometres to a small town called Nyanza, where two sisters agreed to hide us in their home and we survived. ... I would not be here today if it wasn't for those two Hutu sisters.'

After the genocide, women and girls made up 70 per cent of the population, although only 2.3 per cent of genocide suspects were women. Despite their trauma, they had to become heads of households, community leaders and providers, finding homes for 500,000 orphans and producing most of the nation's food. The Government of National Unity, although dominated by a single party, set out to be more inclusive of women and young people. Its policy of decentralising government and setting up local women's councils made it easier for women to get involved in politics.

The new constitution calls for at least 30 per cent of all formal decision-making posts, including seats in the upper and lower chambers of parliament, to be held by women. Many women also stood against, and beat, men for other seats in the lower chamber, bringing the proportion to over 49 per cent.

The international community was concerned by allegations of vote-rigging and intimidation by the dominant party, the Rwandan Patriotic Front, and it will be interesting to see if and how the involvement of large numbers of women will change the way politics works in Rwanda. As MP Connie Bwiza points out: 'It didn't come on a silver plate. Rwandan women have never been involved in politics per se. But today, women have got their own opinions, right from the top to the lower levels. They expect a lot.' Not all grassroots women are convinced the women MPs will make much difference. 'We just elect them but they don't come here and ask us what our problems are and how they can help us,' said Yvonne Owimana, a mother of four and a seamstress in a village outside Kigali. 'They don't have time to come and approach us.' But according to a female vendor in Kigali's main market: 'The women who are representing us have helped us to get our equal rights, like men. Men now know that even we women can do something to improve our country.'[14]

been excluded from politics at any level in India, so this was a huge change.

Many NGOs rallied round to support the new, inexperienced female representatives, including the Confederation of Voluntary Associations (COVA) in Hyderabad, in the south of India. COVA was especially concerned about Muslim and Dalit women, and those from scheduled castes, all marginalised groups in Indian society. A major problem was that most of the women in the new seats were actually 'proxy candidates' for men, often husbands, brothers or other male relatives. The Indian quota system is set up in such a way that male representatives who may have held seats for years suddenly see them taken away because they are reserved for women. A common response, backed by their political parties, is to put forward a puppet woman candidate whom they control; it makes a mockery of the system. COVA decided to try to help women representatives from subordinated groups and castes to become political representatives in their own right, rather than acting as fronts for men. As an illustration of the scale of the problem, 14 of the 18 women representatives involved in their programme had either a husband or a brother active in politics.

COVA supported women office holders in six districts by running workshops for them twice a year. The three-day workshops were designed to give the women a better understanding of local government procedures, public speaking and how to deal with local officials and the media. Between the workshops, COVA monitored the women as they put their new skills into practice. COVA staff talked to the people the women interacted with as politicians to see if their performance, and people's perceptions of them, were changing. The workshops also had the effect of building solidarity among female representatives, which they badly needed in the face of the two-thirds male majority, often hostile, that they faced at council meetings.

The training had a noticeable impact. For the first time, the women started to meet constituents without being accompanied by a male relative. They also started to talk to government officials, make speeches at council meetings and give media interviews on their own initiative. In short, they started to see themselves as politicians in their own right rather than as proxies for men. In some councils, the women representatives were able to band together to get practical arrangements changed in their favour, for instance fixing meeting times that fitted in better with childcare and domestic work, sitting together as a block for mutual support, and obtaining a separate office for women representatives to protect them from harassment.

For Feroze Begum, COVA's workshops changed the way she saw herself. She had been propelled into a seat on a municipal corporation by her husband's business partner, an important figure in the local political scene:

> After victory I did not know about my role or responsibilities. I used to go once every month to the corporation meeting, sign the attendance register and come back. I never went into the field or met the voters. I used to be afraid. For the first six months after getting elected I did not speak at all in the corporation meetings. After the training I gained confidence and got up one day and spoke about the drainage problem in my constituency. Next day the papers reported my speech and I felt very happy to read my name in the newspapers. I find many changes in myself. I do not want to go back to housework or even to teaching. I want to continue in politics.

Opposition from the women's families has been a problem. It came up right from the start, when the families of several women representatives refused to allow them to attend the workshops. Even some of the families which had allowed women to attend workshops, perhaps sending male relatives with them to the first one to 'keep an eye on things', subsequently objected when the women started to fulfil their political duties; this had never been part of the plan. According to one of the representatives, Sujatha, 'After I got elected my family said there is no need to go the municipality and I should concentrate on the housework. They admonished me by saying "don't think you have developed horns just because you got elected."'

However, one of COVA's workshops for male relatives had a positive effect on her brother: 'Now his attitude has changed. He says "it is your post," and he has decided not to interfere with my work.'

The women COVA is supporting have limited autonomy due to lack of mobility, heavy domestic responsibilities and deeply held ideas about what women can and cannot do. Despite the barriers, though, the programme has had some success in challenging the view that women have no place in politics. At the second workshop, few of the women saw a future for themselves in politics, but by the time the fourth workshop came round, most wanted to continue in the political careers that had been thrust upon them. Their sense of having a right to take part in politics, together with their new confidence and skills, also changed the attitudes of constituents, local government officials, journalists and political parties, who are now less likely to see them as fronts for men.[15]

6
Women's economic rights in a globalising world

International trade could help to bolster poor women's economic rights. All too often though, aggressive and unjust trade liberalisation policies interact with the discrimination poor women already face to perpetuate and worsen their poverty. Where trade offers women new opportunities, as with the growth of export manufacturing in Asia, women have little option but to endure severe exploitation; it is the only chance many have to earn an independent wage. Meanwhile, the scandal of commodity dumping by the United States and the European Union has brought deprivation for millions of poor farmers, including women. International development aid organisations, campaign groups and local NGOs are working in different ways to support poor women's economic rights in today's harsh trade environment.

> The question we need to ask is not whether trade liberalisation is good or bad for women as a group, but how trade policy can contribute to the achievement of human rights for everyone and promote sustainable development in all societies.
>
> Association for Women's Rights
> in Development[1]

Globalisation, trade and economic rights

Our world is being globalised – fast. National economies are becoming more closely locked into the global economic system. The type of economic globalisation we are experiencing today (see Box 6.1) is dictated by rich-country governments and transnational companies, and is shaped in their interests. Poor women in the global South help to drive the global economy through both their paid and unpaid work, but millions see their ability to claim their economic rights and make a decent living undermined.

A glance at world poverty figures indicates that some regions are gaining more out of globalisation than others. The proportion of people living in poverty has fallen quite dramatically in Asia, and there has been a small reduction in Latin America. In sub-Saharan Africa, on the other hand, the pro-

Box 6.1: What is globalisation?

Globalisation is an economic process at its heart, although it is politically driven. It also has far-reaching cultural and social ramifications, and is supported by rapid technological innovation, especially in information and communications. Broadly speaking, economic globalisation is characterised by two trends.

Structural adjustment

In pursuit of neo-liberal economic policies of deregulation and privatisation, governments withdraw from interventions that might affect the functioning of free markets, for instance removing subsidies and price controls on food. Government-provided services such as health, education and water sectors are privatised or subsidies are reduced or removed. The introduction of primary school fees in developing countries in the 1980s, which has depressed girls' enrolment, is an example of this trend. Structural adjustment has been the dominant policy agenda in the UK and the United States since the 1980s. The World Bank and the International Monetary Fund (IMF) are at best encouraging, and at worst coercing, developing countries along the same path, making development aid conditional on their adoption of neo-liberal economic policies.

Trade liberalisation

This involves removal of barriers to international trade, such as tariffs and import quotas, and the prioritisation of export production. Some experts argue that the subsequent loss of tariff revenue to developing country governments has been partly responsible for their public spending cuts. Trade liberalisation started to speed up in 1995, with the creation of the World Trade Organization (WTO). Countries in the global South are being encouraged to follow this route, by a combination of the WTO, backed by the EU and the United States, and, again, the influence of the World Bank and IMF.

portion has actually increased and, what is more, the average income of the region's poorest people has fallen.[2] It is generally accepted that the majority of the world's poor people are women, so this is a matter of women's economic rights. Critics like Oxfam, Women in Development Europe (WIDE) and DAWN argue that we need a different type of globalisation, one that is in keeping with world development goals and puts the economic rights of the world's poorest women and men centre-stage. In this chapter, I will briefly look at just one dimension of the globalisation process in relation to poor women in the global South: international trade liberalisation.

Trade liberalisation started to bite during the 1990s. It affects poor women in the global South in many different ways, depending on where they live, their livelihoods, education levels, access to resources such as land and information, and their domestic responsibilities. More than 800 million women are economically active worldwide, in agriculture, small and micro-enterprises and, increasingly, in the export-processing industries.[3] Some are benefiting, others have to struggle even harder than before, and many are completely marginalised from changes which, in theory, could help them to make a living. But they all have something in common. As women, they all experience direct and indirect discrimination that constrains their efforts to claim their economic rights by taking up the opportunities that liberalised trade might offer, and so makes it harder for them to lift themselves and their families out of poverty.

You may not have even realised that women had economic rights. This could be because the international community has never taken economic rights as seriously as civil and political rights. The International Convention on Economic, Social and Cultural Rights (ICESCR) is worded more weakly than its sister convention on civil and political rights, for instance. However, states that have signed the ICESCR are committed to ensuring that it applies to women and men equally. Between them, CEDAW and the BPFA cover various aspects of women, poverty and the economy, including the special situation of rural women. Focusing on paid work, the International Labour Organization (ILO) has issued a Declaration on Fundamental Principles and Rights at Work, which includes equality and freedom of association. The ILO wants to establish a basic 'social floor' for the global economy below which standards cannot drop, countering what it sees as an erosion of dignity and an increase in abusive labour practices.[4]

How discrimination against women perpetuates poverty

In the struggle to earn a livelihood for themselves and their families, poor women in developing countries face profound, often unacknowledged, discrimination as women.

Women's unpaid work is not recognised

Women in the global South, as elsewhere, do a vast amount of unpaid work. This includes domestic and 'care' work, such as cooking, cleaning, childcare and looking after sick relatives, subsistence agriculture, and collecting water, fuel and wild food (see Box 1.6 for an account of the time spent by one woman, Jamal Khatoon, fetching water every day). All this unpaid work makes huge demands on women's time and energy, yet it tends to be taken for granted, perhaps precisely because it is something women do for free. Feminist development economists like Professor Diane Elson have pointed out that the time women spend in this unpaid work is left out of national accounts, labour force surveys and other types of economic analysis. The results are budgets and economic policies that ignore much of the work women do, and so perpetuate discrimination against them.

Women are pushed into informal, unregulated work

In most parts of the global South, jobs for women are few and far between, especially in rural areas. In any case, women's unpaid domestic and childcare responsibilities restrict both the amount and type of paid work they can take on, and many are handicapped in the job market by their low educational levels. The result is that most women workers in the global South are small traders, casual labourers, cleaners, home-workers doing piece-work, unpaid workers in family enterprises and so on; in economists' terminology, they work in the 'informal sector'. Often, this informal work will be combined with subsistence farming. About 60 per cent of women workers in developing countries (apart from North Africa) are in the informal sector, not counting agricultural work.[5] If agricultural work were included, the figure would be much higher. In general, informal work is inferior to paid employment in that earnings are lower and more irregular, working conditions are worse, there is less security and there are no benefits such as pensions or sick leave; see Box 6.2, on how two Angolan women are making a difficult and precarious living.

Women face discrimination in the job market

In recent decades women's share of formal, paid jobs has increased in almost all regions of the world. However, women are still concentrated in jobs associated with their traditional roles as carers and providers, such as nursing, teaching or cleaning, or with imputed feminine characteristics such as 'nimble fingers', the patience to do repetitive tasks all day, and docility. Such work tends to be seen as low-skilled, perhaps because women often do this type of work as part of their unpaid domestic responsibilities. As a result, it is under valued and badly paid. Overall, the income of the world's women is half that of men.

Although detailed figures are hard to come by, evidence suggests that wage gaps between women and men persist even where international trade has created new jobs for women; see Box 6.3, which shows pay gaps by region. Discrimination against women in the job market contributes to world poverty; of the world's 550 million 'working poor', an estimated 330 million are women.[6]

Women working on export fruit farms in South Africa and Chile are at the end of global supply chains that stretch to

Box 6.2: Women in Angola's informal sector[7]

Adelina N'Soma is an Angolan widow in her sixties or seventies. She is very thin, with a bandaged hand. She makes a living making and selling charcoal:

'I cut and burn the wood to make the charcoal, and then I carry it here, ten kilometres. I can sell a bag of charcoal for 25 kwanzas (about $0.40). I might spend 20 kwanzas on maize meal and five on some fish or vegetables. I can only bring one bag of charcoal to sell in a week. The younger people, who are stronger, can make and carry more than I can. Right now, I can't do anything at all, because I cut my hand when I was chopping wood for the charcoal.'

Still in Angola, Rebekah is a young street vendor in the town of Huambo. Perhaps because she is younger, she is doing rather better than Mrs N'Soma. She sells baskets of strawberries:

'We buy the strawberries from the plantation and we buy the baskets from women in the market. We sell a basket for 50 kwanzas. On a good day, we can make between 100 and 200 kwanzas profit. I am trying to find a better job, maybe something in an office. But for now, this is the best thing I can do.'

supermarkets in Europe and North America; here there is plenty of evidence of pay gaps between men and women. On farms in South Africa's Cape Province, which supply Europe's supermarkets, women prune, sort and pack the fruit, all tasks that are paid less than the irrigation, driving

Box 6.3: Women's income as a proportion of men's, by region

Region	Average income of women as percentage of men's
East Asia & Pacific	0.59
Europe	0.57
Central Asia	0.63
Latin America & Caribbean	0.43
Middle East & North Africa	0.33
South Asia	0.47
Sub-Saharan Africa	0.56
North America	0.63
Total	0.52

Source: 'No Country Treats its Women the Same as its Men: The Gender Equity Index – A New Perspective,' *Social Watch*, August 2005, p. 74 <www.socialwatch.org/en/noticias/noticia_117.htm>.

and supervisory jobs men tend to be given. It is a similar story on Chile's export fruit farms too, where female casual workers earn on average only 76 per cent of the equivalent men's wage.[8] Maria, a Chilean grape-picker, told an Oxfam researcher: 'There are many bosses who say "You can't earn more because you are a woman. What do you want money for? It's the man who has to earn more."'[9]

Women face discrimination in property rights

For most poor women, their labour is the only asset they have. This is because in many countries property and inheritance laws, as well as customary practices, seriously discriminate against them, restricting their rights to the land they live and

work on, as well as to other types of property. In parts of southern and eastern Africa, for instance, traditions about inheritance became distorted during the colonialist period, giving rise
to a situation where, today, women are effectively barred from
owning land or other productive assets except as the wives or
mothers of males. Despite their obligations under CEDAW, few
countries have introduced inheritance laws that enable women
to claim their rights to land. And even where the law and
government policy is favourable to women owning land, as in
Vietnam, in practice their rights are ignored. Only 12 per cent
of land-use certificates in Vietnam are in women's names, and
these are mainly single women or widows. In Brazil the figure
is just under 13 per cent, and in Uganda only 7 per cent of land
is owned by women.[10] Women's lack of property rights in turn
affects their chances of obtaining credit, because few poor
women have the collateral required.

Women and girls face discrimination in education

Women in the global South generally have lower education
levels than men and are less likely to receive any vocational
training. In their struggles to make a living, over 500 million
women are handicapped by illiteracy (see Chapter 7 for more
on this).

How trade liberalisation is harming poor women

The dice are loaded against poor women in the global South,
and this inequality between poor men and women is com-
pounded by grotesque inequality between rich and poor
nations. Trade liberalisation is widening this inequality,
because it is the rich countries setting the policy agenda. Of
course, women's experiences of the international trade system

are very diverse. For instance, African and Central American women farmers hit by agricultural 'dumping' could not be more different at first sight from young women working in Asia's export factories. But they are alike in that they show how rapid and aggressive trade liberalisation is damaging the already weak ability of many poor women to exercise their economic rights.

Women farmers hit by commodity dumping

The 'dumping' of artificially low-priced commodities from the EU and the United States on developing countries is probably trade liberalisation at its ugliest. It has destroyed the livelihoods of millions of poor women, men and children involved in farming. For instance, imports of subsidised commodities from the North have caused severe deprivation to farmers, including women, in West and Central Africa and Central America (see Box 6.4).[11] Dumping happens because farmers in the global North, mainly agribusinesses, receive heavy government subsidies; surplus produce is then off-loaded to developing countries at prices far below the actual cost of production. Agricultural dumping undermines poor women's economic rights in several ways. For one thing, women do much of the world's farming, either as unpaid workers on family plots or on their own account; in Africa, for instance, women's work accounts for an estimated 80 per cent of agriculture and food production.[12] And if family income from cash crops falls because of dumping, women have to work all the harder to compensate.

During WTO talks in December 2005, developing countries banded together to demand reforms of the EU and US agricultural regimes, but made little progress in the face of Northern governments' intransigence. According to Oxfam, the meeting was 'a lost opportunity to make trade fairer for poor people around the world.'[13]

Box 6.4: How dumping impacts on women farmers in Africa and Central America

In Ghana, imports of subsidised rice from the United States are having a devastating effect, and women farmers are among the victims. In 2005, British TV presenter June Sarpong travelled to Ghana for Oxfam. There she met about 30 rice farmers, mostly women, who had had to leave their land because they could not get a fair price for their rice. The United States subsidises its rice farmers to the tune of 72 per cent of the cost of production, which means a tonne of rice that costs $200 to produce can be sold for just over $100.[14] Ghanaian farmers just cannot compete with such artificially low prices.

It is a similar story in Mexico. Under the North American Free Trade Agreement (NAFTA), Mexico has opened its markets to imports from the United States, including maize. As a result, US maize exports to Mexico have increased threefold since the early 1990s and now account for about a third of Mexico's maize market. As imports have surged, prices have plummeted; real prices for Mexican maize have fallen more than 70 per cent since 1994. US maize has a huge advantage in the market because it receives big government subsidies. The US maize sector is the largest single recipient of US government payments, receiving $10.1 billion, ten times more than the whole Mexican agricultural budget.

As men have migrated for work and prices for agricultural produce have fallen, women have had to work harder on family plots and in the informal sector, trying to compensate for the drops in income and the loss of men's labour at home. One young woman, Paquita, told a researcher how she had to work on her family's corn plot in Salto de Agua, near San Cristobal: 'I got up at 3 a.m. to make tortillas and left the house at 6 to work on the plot until 3–4 p.m. When I returned home I washed and continued with my work grinding corn and preparing tortillas – there is no rest.'[15]

Women-headed households have been hit the hardest. Their plots tend to be too small for them to get involved in growing vegetables and crops for export to the United States, which is what the Mexican government hoped would happen through NAFTA. In 2000, 56 per cent of women farmers owned less than two hectares of land, compared with 35 per cent of male farmers. And in rural areas, women heads of household tend to have few marketable skills and low education levels, limiting their chances of doing anything other than farming. Between 1992 and 2000, poverty in Mexico's women-headed households increased by 50 per cent.[16]

Women in Asia's export factories

The value of world exports almost doubled between 1993 and 2003 and developing countries' share in these exports surged.[17] Most of this increased share comes from the sweatshops and assembly lines of China and East Asia, where many workers are young, single women, usually migrants from rural areas. They are ideal fodder for the worldwide production networks that characterise today's trade in electronic goods, textiles and garments, providing cheap and flexible labour. Asia's export manufacturing workforce has become 'feminised', and this has gone hand-in-hand with a move to insecure work rather than permanent jobs. In China's Guangdong province, one of the world's fastest-growing industrial areas, 60 per cent of women garment workers have no written contract and 90 per cent have no social insurance.[18] Meanwhile, women working in manufacturing in other parts of the world, such as

Peru, Mozambique and Morocco, have either lost their jobs altogether or been forced into inferior, informal work due to the increased competition that trade liberalisation has brought.

Make no mistake, women in Asia and elsewhere desperately want the jobs that are on offer. They have few, if any, other options and they need the income, both to support their families and because earning a wage can be very empowering for women. Dong, for instance, is a young Chinese woman who left her village in one of China's poorest rural areas to work in an export factory on the coast. She told a researcher how she wanted to earn some money of her own so that she would have some financial independence when she went back to her village to marry: 'Life will be happy if my husband and my parents-in-law treat me nice. But no one knows. It's better for me to have some money of my own.'[19] See also Box 3.2, on how work in Bangladesh's garment factories has helped thousands of women there to achieve financial independence. The issue is that, rather than having to endure extreme exploitation that takes advantage of their weak bargaining position, women workers should be able to enjoy at least the basic labour rights set out by the ILO.

The reality is that many have little choice but to endure low pay and harsh conditions, due to the absence of effective labour protection and the denial of their right to organise as workers. Chinese law rules out the establishment of independent trade unions, for instance. Women's vulnerability is one of the factors that have enabled the big retailers and brand companies in the global North to compete in what some commentators call a 'race to the bottom' in terms of wages and labour standards. Together with the removal of trade barriers and controls, and improvements in communications and transport, it allows the big retailers and brand companies, such as Wal-Mart in the United States, Tesco in the UK, El Corte Ingles in Spain or world-brand Nike, to shop around for the best deal from all over the world. The firms that supply them, too, are free to move around; the director of a big transnational company has likened the factory of today to 'a ship that drops anchor wherever wage costs are lowest'.[20] Under pressure to maximise short-term profits for their shareholders, retailers and brands demand ever-faster turnaround times for orders, higher quality and lower prices, putting the squeeze on their suppliers and, at the far end of the supply chain, the women making the goods. Factory managers know all too well that, if they refuse an order, or fail to deliver on time, the buyer may go elsewhere and never come back. The graphic description of conditions in a Chinese factory when a 'rush job' is on (Box 6.5), illustrates the impact this business model can have on women's working hours and conditions.

Rather than protecting the rights of their women workers, governments all too often turn a blind eye to labour law violations. In some cases, for example in Bangladesh, Colombia and Nicaragua, they have actually started to weaken labour legislation, so as not to lose out to competitor countries.[21]

Box 6.5: Conditions in a Chinese factory with a rush job

'In order to rush an order through in as little as seven days, from the time of its placement, my working sisters and I are forced to work non-stop for 48 hours. The shop-floor is not well-ventilated and heavy dust particles are virtually everywhere. I feel exhausted and extremely tired. In that single month, we recorded a total of 150 hours overtime, which far exceeded the 36-hour legal limit. I nevertheless got only 70 yuan (approximately US$9) overtime payment. The overtime payment is never made transparent to us. ... Now, the situation is the worst. We haven't received any basic wage for the past two months. How can we survive?'[22]

Reacting to bad publicity and consumer pressure over workers' poor pay and conditions, many large transnational companies have adopted voluntary codes of conduct covering the
treatment of workers. However, it is easy for factory managers
to fake compliance. In any case, critics such as Oxfam argue
that codes can only be effective if based on labour legislation,
and if workers themselves are involved in developing, and
monitoring against, the codes.

Supporting women's struggles for economic rights

Poor women in the global South are organising in various
ways, whether as workers in export enterprises or producers in
their own right. And there are various global or North-based
initiatives assisting them to claim economic rights in the context
of a fiercely competitive world trade system:

◆ At the international policy level, *women's lobbying and
campaign groups*, like WIDE and the International
Gender and Trade Network, lobby the WTO, calling for
an alternative vision of international trade that would
support, rather than damage, women's economic rights.
The WTO's 6th Ministerial Conference in Hong Kong in
December 2005 was accompanied by activists' workshops
and a lively women's march, focusing, among other
things, on how small-scale farmers, street vendors and
handicraft producers lose out in competition with big
transnational companies.[23] Using a different strategy,
Women's Edge Coalition has developed a framework for
analysing the likely impact of national trade policies on
women: the 'Trade Impact Review'.[24]

◆ In addition there are various *trade campaigns and anti-
sweatshop campaigns*, such as the Clean Clothes Campaign
in Europe, Labour Behind the Label and Women Working

Worldwide in the UK, and United Students Against Sweat-shops in the United States. Some of the big international NGOs, such as Oxfam, are also lobbying and campaigning on trade issues. All these organisations are supporting women workers' organisations in the South, putting pressure on international policy bodies, governments and transnational companies, and helping to publicise the issues.

◆ There are many *fair trade initiatives* enabling producers, including women, to get a better deal from trade with the global North. Kuapa Kokoo, a Ghanaian cocoa farmers' co-operative, is especially interesting because it has empowered women farmers; some are now shareholders in the UK-based Day Chocolate Company.

◆ There are also thousands of *small NGOs and community-based organisations* helping women to take advantage of the opportunities that international trade can offer, for instance through training and collective negotiation with buyers. As an example, organisations in Chile have supported women who collect seaweed and forest products for export (see Box 6.6).

◆ On the wider issue of integrating women's unpaid work into economic analysis, the South Africa Women's Budget Initiative has led the way in carrying out '*gender audits*' of budgets and policies. Similar work is now being done in about 50 other countries.

◆ Oxfam is *challenging sex segregation* in the labour market, albeit in a small way, by employing women to work on their development and humanitarian projects in traditional 'men's roles', like driving and building.[25]

The story that follows, of women workers' struggle for rights in an Indonesian factory, is an interesting example of an alliance involving organisations in both North and South. It shows how globalisation can work to support women's economic rights, rather than undermine them.

Box 6.6: Helping women in Chile's informal sector to organise[26]

In Caleta Tumbles, Chile, women's main source of income is collecting seaweed. Local NGO Ana Clara, which at this time was supported by Oxfam, helped the women to organise a union, the Seaweed Collectors' Union, which went on to negotiate a collective agreement with an export company. The agreement guaranteed them a price almost double what they had received before. In other areas, women depend on collecting forest products like bark, roots, mushrooms and berries. They sell them to intermediaries who supply export companies. The products end up in cosmetics, processed food, teas and medicines in use all over the world. In VIII Region, NGO Taller de Acción Cultural, another former local Oxfam partner, has helped groups of women plant collectors to organise.

On another level, Oxfam is helping women workers in Chile's informal sector to lobby regional government. The women want to be officially recognised as workers, which would give them access to health care, education and training, and social security.

Kicking back against labour rights abuses

Workers at PT Panarub, a West Javanese factory producing Adidas football boots, have been resisting low pay, forced overtime and other labour rights abuses for years. With the help of an alliance between a local union, Indonesian NGOs and anti-sweatshop campaigners in the global North, in mid-2005 they were able to start to claim their labour rights.

In 2005, there were 11,500 workers at PT Panarub, 80 per

cent of them women. The Australian NGO Oxfam Community Aid Abroad (OCAA), now Oxfam Australia, included the factory in its 2002 report, *We Are Not Machines*. The report documented labour rights abuses in factories producing sports shoes for both Nike and Adidas. Among other things, wages (the equivalent of US$1.65 per day) were very low, so that most workers, many of whom were internal migrants, could not afford to have their children living with them. Working hours were extremely long, with forced overtime, and supervisors often shouted at and insulted workers who they deemed were too slow. Women in Indonesia have a legal right to take time off work during their periods. But at Panarub, workers who needed this unpaid leave were subjected to a humiliating physical examination in the factory clinic; this was such a deterrent that, in effect, they were denied this legal right.

We Are Not Machines also publicised the management's repeated attempts to repress an independent union, Gabungan Serikat Buruh Independen (GSBI). In particular, OCAA campaigned against the arrest and imprisonment of a GSBI official, Ngadinah Binti Abu Mawardi, who in 2001 was held in prison for a month and subjected to a lengthy trial after helping to organise a strike. Most of the workers had joined the strike, demanding, among other things, to be paid for overtime at the legally mandated rate and to be able to take their menstrual leave without being examined. Arrested at the request of Panarub management, Ngadinah was charged under Article 160 (Inciting Others to Break the Law) and Article 335 (Unpleasant Conduct Towards Others) of the Indonesian criminal code.

Thanks to OCAA and other international organisations, Ngadinah's trial received a lot of media attention both at home and abroad. The charge of 'Unpleasant Conduct' aroused particular concern, because this vaguely defined offence was often used to quash strikes by former President Suharto's repressive regime. Ngadinah herself said in a statement: 'employers and government officials are colluding to suppress legitimate union activities'. She told the judge at her trial that the strike was not due to her, but rather to an outbreak of worker frustration that had built up after years of low pay, forced overtime and abuse: 'If we don't reach our target the management gets very angry with us. Angry to the point that sometimes they throw shoes at the workers.'

Thanks to the international publicity generated by OCAA and other local and international campaigning organisations, Ngadinah was eventually found not guilty, and PT Panarub stopped persecuting GSBI members with harsh treatment and the imposition of menial tasks. On the other hand, OCAA continued to receive reports from GSBI that the union was being discriminated against in other ways. After OCAA lobbied Adidas on the matter, the two parties agreed to invite the US-based Worker Rights Consortium (WRC) to investigate the allegations of labour rights infringements. WRC's subsequent report both verified GSBI's claims and drew attention to serious health and safety problems. Workers suffered regular burns from hot glue machines, inhaled harmful rubber fumes throughout their working day, and risked losing fingers through dangerous machinery.

After the publication of the report, Adidas and Panarub management acted on most of WRC's recommendations, re-hiring GSBI union officials who had been sacked, moving to make all jobs in the factory permanent and, with the help of a new company doctor, initiating health and safety reforms. Women no longer have to endure a physical examination when they claim menstrual leave. Unfortunately, in October 2005, management at Panarub dismissed the leaders of one of the unions, and since then, conditions in the factory have deteriorated once again – although those dismissed workers are now being paid a 'hardship allowance'.

For Timothy Connor, who specialises in labour rights for Oxfam Australia, workers' right to join an independent union is the key issue in factories such as Panarub. He summarises the 2005 improvements like this:

> There is more space for women and men to claim their legal rights, their workplace is safer and they have greater income security. The struggle of Panarub workers is well known throughout the local area, and it would be interesting to see what impact it has had on other workers' campaigns.

He points out that these positive outcomes did not come about overnight, but on the contrary have followed years of struggle and painstaking work:

> The most important contributing factor has been the courage and determination of the workers themselves, who risked their livelihoods to join an independent union. Also, they have been supported by several different organisations working closely together. For instance, many GSBI officials were originally trained in labour rights issues by one of our Indonesian partner organisations, the Social Information and Legal Guidance Foundation. The Clean Clothes Campaign in Germany were allies too; they used *We Are Not Machines* as evidence in an official complaint to the Organisation of Economic Co-operation and Development, which has a code of conduct for transnational companies. And in the last analysis, Adidas' decision to protect its reputation by inviting in an independent investigator was very constructive.[27]

The most important outstanding issue is that Adidas is not yet willing to give Panarub a financial incentive to respect labour rights. Oxfam Australia are continuing to campaign on this case.[28]

7
'Sowing a seed': the right to education

The right to education was laid down in the 1940s, and girls' right to an education has been reiterated in international treaties and agreements regularly since then. Today, however, one in every five girls of primary-school age does not go to school. There are also wide gaps between the proportions of girls and boys getting through secondary school. Abolishing school fees is a good strategy for improving enrolment figures, but measures that address girls' particular needs are also essential for improving girls' enrolment and the proportion actually completing a basic education. Improvements such as wiping out sexual harassment in schools and providing amenities such as clean toilets should be the first priority, while girls also have a right to an education that builds their self-esteem and fully develops their abilities. Meanwhile, two-thirds of the world's illiterate adults are women. Expanding funding for women's adult literacy classes would help women to exercise their rights in many spheres, and would speed progress on development goals.

> Education has sown a seed in me, which is growing and flowering to produce other seeds, the seed of lifting the value of girls and women in the communities around me. I now understand that women can be recognised as important people in the community, and I can communicate freely, bringing all my views and discussing them with people, even those in high positions.
>
> Esther Jena, a young business administrator[1]

Esther Jena's words vividly express the empowering potential of education for girls. The right to education was first set out in the UDHR in 1948, and the Convention on the Rights of the Child reaffirmed it 'on the basis of equal opportunity'. Yet, in 2001/02, the latest year for which statistics are available at the time of writing, 115 million primary-age children did not go to school for even one day. Sixty-two million, about 53 per cent of them, were girls. Put another way, about one in five of all girls of primary-school age did not go to school at all. The bar chart in Box 7.1 shows the numbers of out-of-school children of primary age, and the proportion of girls, for each region. Worldwide, 53 per cent of out of school children are

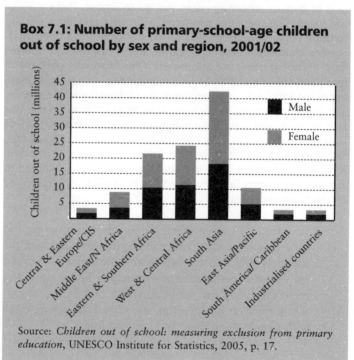

Box 7.1: Number of primary-school-age children out of school by sex and region, 2001/02

Source: *Children out of school: measuring exclusion from primary education*, UNESCO Institute for Statistics, 2005, p. 17.

girls, but in the Middle East and North Africa, South Asia and West and Central Africa, the proportion is higher.[2] The legacy of denying girls their right to education in the past is that about two-thirds of the world's estimated 771 million illiterate adults are women.[3]

Enrolment is a necessary first step, but of course, girls' right to an education is about more than 'bums on seats'. It also concerns what girls learn and how it equips them for the future. What happens to the girls who do get to primary school? Sadly, not all of them have the same positive experience as Esther Jena:

◆ Many girls have poor attendance, for a variety of reasons including demands for their labour at home.

◆ More girls than boys drop out before they have got four or five years of schooling, the minimum needed for a basic education.

◆ Millions of children receive poor-quality education with outdated and irrelevant content, untrained teachers, a dearth of basic resources and dilapidated, uncomfortable school buildings.

◆ All too often, the curriculum, learning materials and teachers' behaviour discriminate against girls, reinforcing negative stereotypes about women's roles, and discouraging them from aspiring to be anything other than wives and mothers.

◆ Various studies suggest that, for thousands of girls in Africa and Asia, sexual harassment by fellow-students and teachers is part and parcel of their school experience.

The international community currently has a commitment to eliminating gender disparity in primary and secondary education, the target for MDG3. Yet, when, in 2005, it became clear that the target had been missed, the failure was not even mentioned in the final document of that year's UN World Summit.

That is the big picture, and it is quite a depressing one. Personally, I find figures like '62 million out-of-school girls', hard to grasp. A close-up can say more than a panorama, and when I visited a centre for out-of-school girls in Nigeria in 2004, it helped me to understand what the figures mean in human terms (Box 7.2).

As well as being a tragedy for girls themselves and a denial of their rights, depriving them of a decent education has terrible consequences for the societies they live in. Educating girls is generally recognised as the key to reducing poverty in low-income countries because of its economic and social multiplier effects. The world's failure to hit the MDG3 target is momentous, in part because it jeopardises the other MDGs too. MDG2 aims for universal primary education by 2015, which is now unlikely, while the world desperately needs educated women in order to meet other targets such as reducing child mortality, improving maternal health and combating HIV/AIDS and malaria.[4] From a purely economic point of view, countries with big gaps between the numbers of girls and boys going to school have lower gross national product and economic growth than those where roughly equal numbers are enrolled, all other things being equal.[5] The human development gains of educating girls include lower birth-rates, and lower maternal and infant mortality (Box 7.3).

These are instrumental arguments; in other words, they show what girls' education can do for society at large rather than the girls themselves. Compelling though they are, it is important to remember that girls' education is a right rather than a means to an end, however worthwhile that end may be. As well as being important in itself, it is an 'enabling right'. In other words, women who have received some education are in a better position to exercise rights in other areas of their lives. For instance, they are more likely to achieve their economic rights by getting decent jobs, running their own businesses and being able to deal with money. This might mean something as simple as not being

Box 7.2: Truancy in reverse in Nigeria

There are an estimated 7 million children in Nigeria out of school, 62 per cent of whom are girls. In 2004, I met 15 such girls, aged 7–17 years, in Damaturu, Yobe province. They were learning to knit in a dilapidated shelter, part of an informal education centre for girls who do not go to school. They told me that their families were poor, and some said their parents disapproved of sending girls to the government schools because they would have to mix with boys. Instead, their mothers sent them out hawking every day; in this region, hawking is a traditional way for girls to contribute to the family income and earn the dowries they need when they get older.

After a couple of hours selling matches and other sundries, they come to the centre between 8am and noon, often without their parents' knowledge. In the afternoon they take their wares back on the streets, and finally go home to help with the chores. At the centre, they learn practical skills such as knitting and sewing, but above all they come for the literacy classes. They yearn to be able to read and write, which is why they are prepared to defy their parents by slipping away to the centre. One told me how she had begged her parents to send her to school, but they had refused; she did not know why.

Although their futures are likely to be early marriage and pregnancy, the girls all had other aspirations. Several told me they wanted to become teachers, nurses or government workers, reflecting both their ambitions and the limited range of role models they had been exposed to.

Box 7.3: Human development gains from girls' education

◆ In Zimbabwe, only 17 per cent of the girls supported through secondary school by the Campaign for Female Education (CAMFED International) become mothers by the age of 24, compared with a national average of 47 per cent.

◆ A recent study across 65 low and middle-income countries found that doubling the proportion of girls educated at secondary school level would reduce the infant mortality rate by more than 50 per cent.[6]

◆ According to Save the Children, babies born to mothers who have been to primary school are twice as likely to live beyond five years of age, and the world's failure to meet the Millennium Development Goals' target for girls' education will result in a million unnecessary child and maternal deaths each year.[7]

cheated by a market trader because you can do simple sums. Secondary and higher education have especially high pay-offs in terms of empowering women to achieve their rights;[8] for instance, see the story at the end of this chapter on how rural African girls who have been supported through secondary school are leading change in their communities. But in Africa and Asia there are still wide gaps between the proportions of girls and boys getting through secondary school.[9] The interaction between the right to education and women's other rights works both ways. In societies where women's rights are denied across the board, it might seem like an irrelevance or a luxury to send girls to school, rather than a good investment for their future. For instance, if there are few jobs or livelihood opportunities for women, parents may think there is little point. Conversely, in the absence of decent schools, parents may decide to marry their daughters off young, because there are no other options. The story in Box 7.4 suggests that more and better schools would reduce this harmful practice.

Barriers to girls' education

There are many obstacles that prevent so many girls getting an education, and to some extent they vary from place to place. In general, they arise from interactions between poverty, at both household and national level, and discrimination against girls and women. Box 7.5 lists of some of the barriers.

Household poverty is a huge issue, because of the tuition fees and various other costs involved in sending children to school, including: exam fees, PTA contributions, buying uniforms,

Box 7.4: Waramatou's story

Waramatou Harouna was eight in 2001, the year the community school was built in her village of Tchiwol-Sarey, in Niger. Young as she was, her parents had already decided to marry her to a young man in the village. When the school was opened however, they changed their minds and decided to enrol her.

Waramatou's mother subsequently became involved in local-level campaigning against early marriage organised by VIE, the local NGO that had opened the school.

In 2004 Waramatou was chosen by her school to take part in the 'Big Lobby' organised by the Global Campaign for Education. At twelve years old, she took the floor in the Parliament of Niger to deliver a message from her region. VIE says that many girls like her get married off early and become young mothers because there are no schools for them to go to.[10]

Box 7.5: What keeps girls out of school?

Negative cultural and social factors

◆ If they have to choose, parents usually prefer to educate sons rather than daughters.
◆ Girls' early marriage.
◆ Early pregnancy and parents' anxieties about it.
◆ Girls are expected to work in the home.
◆ In some societies, girls are seen as less intelligent than boys.
◆ In rural areas, there are few female 'role models'.

Inadequate school provision

◆ Schools too far away.
◆ Dilapidated buildings.
◆ Lack of school furniture and equipment.
◆ Untrained teachers.
◆ Education not relevant, seen as a waste of time.
◆ Dirty toilets or no toilets at all.
◆ No separate toilets for girls and boys.
◆ Inadequate or no food provided.

Schools' failure to encourage girls

◆ Sexual harassment and abuse by fellow pupils and teachers.
◆ Girls are often expected to do more cleaning at school than boys.
◆ Curricula and books with negative gender stereotypes.
◆ Teachers favour boys in classroom, have low expectations of girls.
◆ Too few women teachers.

lunch money, charges for schoolbooks, transport costs and so on, not to mention the 'opportunity costs' of losing a girl's labour. For low-income families, these can be the biggest items of expenditure they have to make, and can result in girls staying at home (see Box 7.6). If a family is too poor to send all their children to school, it is usually girls who lose out.

The World Bank drastically undermined the right to education when it forced governments in the global South to introduce primary school tuition fees starting in the 1980s, but in recent years the trend has reversed, with dramatic surges in overall enrolment in Malawi, Uganda, Tanzania, Kenya and East Timor after fees were abolished.[11] But experience in Uganda shows that fee abolition, although a very effective strategy for boosting primary enrolment rates, is not enough in itself to close gender gaps in primary education. In 1997, the government in Uganda started to provide free places for four children in every family, stipulating that these should not just be sons if there were also daughters. Enrolment immediately shot up, but while national enrolment figures for girls are fairly good in the first two years of primary school (48 per cent of girls enrolled), after the fourth year the gap starts to widen, with only an estimated 65 per cent

Box 7.6: 'They can only afford to pay for one'

When I grow up I'd like to get a good job but I don't think we'll be able to because we're very poor. My parents have to pay more than 2000 yuan a year for my brother to go to middle school. My grandfather is the village leader, and he gives them to the money to pay for my brother, but they won't be able to afford to pay for me to go too. They'd like both of us to go, but they can't afford it. They can only afford to pay for one.

Li Hongjiao, aged 12, Shuanjiang County,
Yunnan Province, China[12]

of girls completing primary school, compared with 71 per cent of boys.[13] As well as removing fees, governments need to set other measures in place that specifically target girls.

Education is about more than schooling

It is very sad that many children in the global South who manage to enrol in school, sometimes at great cost to their families, find it anything but a rewarding experience. On a visit to a school in northern Nigeria in 2004, I stood outside a primary classroom for over 20 minutes, listening to Grade 1 children chanting the phrase 'human resource development'. The phrase meant nothing to them; apart from anything else, these six-year-olds did not know any English. But it was the title of the next syllabus module, so the teacher, who was probably untrained, had written it on the board and got them to repeat it together over and over as a way of filling in time.

Poor-quality and irrelevant education is one of the reasons why many girls drop out of school after a year or two, before they have had a chance to acquire basic literacy skills. Peru, for instance, had attained equal numbers of girls and boys enrolling by 2000, but in a study of four schools in the Andes, researcher Patricia Ames found that children spent as little as two hours per school-day in learning activities, textbooks were kept in cupboards rather than distributed to the pupils, and teachers regularly asked girl pupils to wash their clothes, do their dishes or look after their babies. It is small wonder that many girls could not see the point of persevering with their 'education', and dropped out after a few years.[14]

As well as being relevant and stimulating, education should boost the confidence, self-esteem and aspirations of girls and boys alike. In the words of the Convention on the Rights of the Child (CRC), it should be directed at 'the development of the child's personality, talents and mental and physical abilities to their fullest potential'.[15] In contrast to this aspiration, it is common to see both the formal and hidden school curricula constraining girls, dampening their self-confidence, limiting their aspirations, and generally 'keeping them in their place'.

By 'hidden curriculum' is meant what children learn from the way teachers and other pupils treat them, and from unspoken messages in books and learning materials. For instance, in many countries it is common to find teachers, both male or female, favouring boy pupils over girls in their classroom interactions, for example choosing boys rather than girls to answer questions and making eye contact only with boys. In many school books, girls and women either hardly feature at all, or are only depicted in ways that reinforce gender stereotypes (Box 7.7). Messages like these are unspoken but can have a big impact on how girls see themselves.

In the worst-case scenario, the hidden curriculum for girls consists of sexual harassment and abuse, coercive sex and even rape, at the hands of teachers and fellow students (Box 7.8).

If education were free for all children, good quality and secure, there would be far fewer girls, or boys for that matter, out of school in the global South. As far as quality is concerned, at the very least schools should be free of sexual harassment and have

Box 7.7: Negative stereotypes in Pakistan's school books

A recent study in Pakistan found that 74 per cent of characters portrayed in textbooks were men and boys with only 26 per cent women or girls, usually pictured in weak roles. Girls tended to be shown doing menial jobs, confined in their houses, whereas boys were shown in the public sphere. In the few cases where women were shown outside the home, their lives were depicted as difficult and undesirable. Any professional women characters were given names like Mary or Carol, rather than Muslim names.[16]

Box 7.8: Danger and harassment at school

All the touching at school, in class, in the corridors, all day everyday bothers me. Boys touch your bum, your breasts. Some teachers will tell the boys to stop and they may get a warning or detention, but it doesn't work. Other teachers just ignore it. You won't finish your work because they are always pestering you the whole time.[17]

In 2005, ActionAid International launched a campaign based on studies in twelve countries in Africa and Asia. Their studies found that violence against girls occurs in, around and on the way to and from school and takes many forms including rape, sexual harassment, intimidation, aggressive teasing and threats.

Although the problem tends to peak during their adolescence, younger girls suffer too. In itself, this is a violation of their rights. It also damages their ability to exercise their other rights by contributing to low enrolment, poor performance at school, high drop-out rates, teenage pregnancy, early marriage (which parents often think of as insurance against the 'shame' of early pregnancy) and HIV/AIDS, and causes lifelong psychological damage to girls.

In Mozambique, Oxfam partner Association for Gender and Education (AMME) has achieved a notable success in its programme to end sexual abuse of girls in school. In 2004, a schoolgirl in the village of Lioma, Gurue district, became pregnant and denounced her teacher, who it turned out had sexually abused several other girls too. AMME helped villagers to take the case to a local tribunal, but the District Education Department did nothing. So AMME took the case to the Provincial Department of Education, which eventually dismissed the teacher.

As a result of this lobbying, the national Ministry of Education has passed a new ministerial decree which, for the first time, creates a clear procedure for dealing with such cases. AMME has publicised the new legislation among teachers, making the point that there is no longer impunity for abusing pupils.[18]

clean, sex-segregated toilets. At the policy and financing levels, the Global Campaign for Education (GCE) has identified four features that are common to countries like Malawi and Bangladesh, where there has been significant progress on girls' education:

◆ The governments concerned have strong political will to get more girls into school.
◆ Government policy pays heed to civil society advice and demands from women's organisations like the Federation of African Women Educationalists.
◆ Comprehensive strategies have been developed that boost demand for girls' education, as well as improving school provision.
◆ Governments and international donors commit to sustained budget increases for education.[19]

For poor countries, guaranteed assistance from the international donor community is essential. Governments need to know that money is available to fund their plans over a five to ten-year timeframe. The Education for All Fast Track Initiative (FTI), which was launched in 2002, was designed to do just that. The promise was that poor countries that developed a credible plan for getting all their children into school would receive international donor funding to help them. Few rich countries have honoured their commitments, though. UNESCO estimates that the 79 low-income countries need $7.1bn a year in aid in order to get all their children into school – a 500 per cent increase in aid compared with 2000 levels.

Although the need for more and better-focused development aid is clear, it would be naïve to think that the shortcomings of education systems in so much of the global South are wholly due to government poverty and rich donor's miserliness. Look at Pakistan, a country that spends only 2.2 per cent of its budget on education, but huge amounts on the military, including nuclear tests. As a consequence, the figures for girls' education are worse in Pakistan than in either Bangladesh or India, although, of the three countries, it has the highest gross national product per capita.[20] At the same time, the fact that 7 million girls are not going to school in Nigeria is linked to the systematic theft of oil revenues worth billions of dollars, squirreled away in Swiss bank accounts by venal and corrupt leaders.

NGOs are responding to inadequate government provision by developing new tactics, tailoring them to address the specific barriers facing girls in different communities (Box 7.9). The challenge they face is how to 'scale up' these initiatives so they make a more significant impact, for instance by influencing mainstream education provision.

Spelling out empowerment: women's literacy

So far this chapter has focused on today's school-age girls, but what about the approximately 500 million adult women who cannot read or write? Many development activists see women's adult literacy as a highly effective strategy for helping women to claim their rights, while also bringing

Box 7.9: Small-scale NGO initiatives on girls' education

NGOs are trying out innovative tactics for improving both access to and the quality of education for girls, responding to local situations. Here is a selection:

◆ In a slum area of Delhi, Shadipur, most girls do not get past the first grades of school. One of the biggest barriers is that mothers need their eldest daughters to look after younger siblings so that they can go to work. Mobile Crèches, an Oxfam partner organisation, provides childcare for about 1,000 households. So now girls from these families can attend school, while at the same time their brothers and sisters get valuable early childhood care.

◆ The Makhi Welfare Organisation in Pakistan has succeeded in schooling almost 200 girls, changing community attitudes to girls' education and influencing the national Education Department. At community meetings, they have played tapes of speeches by a religious leader in which he asks villagers to send their sons and daughters to school, citing Islamic teachings that support girls' education.

◆ The Federation of African Women Educationalists (FAWE) has promoted girls' clubs in several African countries. In Tanzania, FAWE joined forces with the University of Dar es Salaam in 1997 to start Tuseme or 'Let's Speak Out' clubs for secondary-school girls. Girls meet after school to help each other with their homework, analyse problems besetting them and devise potential solutions. Discussions often culminate in a drama performance for teachers and parents, setting out the issues. The clubs usually receive some start-up cash which girls then use to generate more resources, for instance by making and selling soap.

ambitious development goals within reach. Programmes like these are most successful in empowering women when they not only teach reading and writing, but also create a forum for talking about issues that affect them, and planning collective action. This is a model first developed by Paolo Freire in Latin America during the 1960s and 1970s. He invented the term 'conscientisation' to describe the process of helping poor men and women to analyse the structural forces shaping their subordination. Organisations like Nirantar in India give adult literacy for women a specifically feminist slant (Box 7.10).

Working in the Freirean tradition, ActionAid International has developed the 'Reflect' approach to adult literacy, which it describes as combining literacy with social change. Reflect has been influential in changing practices around the world, with over 500 organisations – including governments, NGOs, UN agencies and grassroots social movements – using the approach in over 70 countries. It prioritises the practical use of language to identify and challenge social injustice. Groups are usually mixed-sex, but an average of 80 per cent of participants are women. Many women say Reflect activities make them feel stronger and more confident on an individual level. The process of learning, discussion and reflection in a group seems to work very well at building up a sense of personhood and rights (Box 7.11).

ActionAid International and the GCE are calling for governments to allocate at least 3 per cent of their education budgets to adult literacy, and for international donors to plug any resource gaps, in line with their commitments at the World Education Forum, Dakar, in 2000.[21]

Box 7.10: 'Information is power'

For Nirantar, education is a feminist issue; the organisation defines education for women as 'learning that enables women to take control over their lives'. Nirantar believes that there is a need for reading material for women that demystifies information and deals with women's lived realities: 'a large part of learning is access to information – and information is power.' They are developing teaching approaches specifically suited to women and adolescent girls, as well as resources such as *Pitara*, a bi-monthly Hindi magazine for readers with basic literacy skills that looks at issues in women's everyday lives. The magazine is distributed widely throughout Hindi-speaking India. Among their other activities, Nirantar has also trained and supported a group of women in Chitrakut district of Uttar Pradesh, some with minimal literacy levels, to produce a local newspaper.[22]

Women leading social change in Africa

Young rural women in sub-Saharan Africa are among the most disadvantaged social groups on earth, and a big proportion of the world's out-of-school girls are from this region. The CAMFED Association (CAMA) demonstrates how empowering education can be in this context, with a knock-on effect in terms of other women's rights. The Association was started in Zimbabwe in 1998, by girls who had completed their secondary education with the help of the Campaign for Female Education (CAMFED International), its 'mother' organisation. CAMFED works closely with rural communities to provide support to poor girls in Zimbabwe, Zambia and Ghana, so that they can finish school. The assistance comes in the shape of financial help to individual girls, equipment and learning materials for schools,

Box 7.11: 'Things began to change'[23]

'As we started discussing our problems and how we can find solutions to them through our own efforts, things began to change. We realised that most of our problems were because we were not aware about our fundamental rights! Now we know that we have equal rights with our menfolk. ... We used not to go to the [village council] meetings thinking we had no right to. ... But recently we went and even managed to speak up. We presented the three main problems we were facing – muddy and poor roads in our hamlet, no verandah in the primary school forcing the children to either get burnt in the sun or drenched in the rains. And last of all concrete steps leading to our pond where we can sit and bathe and wash clothes.'

Jagyaseni Muna, member of Reflect circle
in Bubel, a village in Orissa, India

'Before I got involved with the Reflect group I felt out of touch with the world around me, but now I'm learning so much. We women didn't used to sit out with the men, speaking in front of them used to make me nervous, but now I'm in the Reflect group I have more confidence in my own point of view. ... I see some changes starting. It used to be that fetching water was women's work – and people will say that it looks strange to see a man doing it, but my husband sometimes helps out when we go to gather firewood – or he takes care of the children. ... Reflect has helped me to realise that I can make changes in my life.'

Sanatu, member of Reflect circle
in Wayamba village, northern Ghana

and running girls' hostels to cut out the problem of long distances to school.

CAMA has about 3,000 members and more join every year as they finish secondary school. They aim to empower other young women to lead change in their communities. Having all experienced hardship and deprivation themselves, they understand rights issues as they are lived on a daily basis in villages and rural households. After getting through secondary school, they could have just concentrated on bettering their own lives, but many are working to promote other girls' and women's rights in their communities.

The Seed Money Scheme, for instance, gives grants to young rural women for small business start-ups. This means they can become economically independent without having to move to the towns to find work, where they would be exposed to sexual exploitation and HIV/AIDS. The initial grants are complemented by regular business training and mentoring, as well as small loans for expanding their enterprises. In 2003 alone, 310 young women started up small businesses through the scheme, ranging from poultry rearing to hairdressing. But what is really striking is that an impressive number have used the profits from their businesses to support children through school.

Another of CAMA's current priorities is to break the silence around the sexual abuse of girls. They counsel victims and their families, and are raising awareness of the issue with local chiefs, police and the judiciary. In 2003, their campaign reached 40,000 people in ten rural districts, with the direct result that at least 30 cases of abuse were reported to the authorities. CAMA's work with local chiefs on this issue is a good example of its members' confidence and courage. In this part of Africa, chiefs wield great power, and are at the other end of the social scale from young, single women. Yet as a result of their advocacy, a local chief, Chief Mutekedza, has changed the way his traditional courts deal with child sex abuse cases: 'After realising the number of sensitive questions brought to my court and how shy most girls were to disclose information of an intimate nature, I appointed a woman assessor.' This is an example of the kind of change in local laws and policies that CAMA is achieving. Chief Mutekedza is now talking to other chiefs about making rural communities safer for girls.

CAMA's 308 Ghanaian members are all based in the northern region of the country. They are speaking out about two practices that harm girls: street-portering and fostering. Working as street porters exposes young girls to sexual exploitation from lorry-drivers travelling through the district to the coastal ports. Fostering turns girls into Cinderellas; all too often it is a disguised form of child labour that prevents them from attending school. Yvonne Kapenza now runs a successful small business selling vegetables and other products and is supporting her younger brothers through school. But she remembers how she was fostered out to her uncle's family: 'At the age of six, some children were already attending their primary school but as for me, it was a different story, I was staying at home as a baby-minder, housemaid and cattle-herder.' Many CAMA activists have had similar experiences, so they are challenging families to give fostered girls the same food, health care and education as other children in extended households.

CAMA's members are living proof of the link between girls' right to education and other human rights. Nothing can express that better than a CAMA Ghana member articulating the determination and inner strength she has found: 'Let us declare war against HIV/AIDS, teenage pregnancy, malnutrition and early marriage. We will turn the stones the older generation could not.'[24]

8
The violence against women pandemic

Violence against women occurs on a vast scale and takes different forms throughout women's lives, ranging from sex-selective
abortions to abuse of the elderly. It is a women's human rights
issue, as well as a public health concern and a drag on development. Domestic violence is the commonest form of violence
against women and there is a loosely organised movement of
organisations addressing it, including a few men's organisations.
During recent conflicts in Bosnia, the Democratic Republic of
Congo, Darfur and elsewhere, rape has been used systematically
as a weapon of war. In 1998, the establishment of the International Criminal Court, aimed at bringing perpetrators to justice,
was a huge breakthrough for women's rights activists.

Writing about violence against women is disturbing. It is
partly the scale of it. Although a lot goes unreported, small
studies in various countries give us piecemeal glimpses of a
shocking 'big picture', with millions of women's lives
blighted by domestic violence alone; see Box 8.1. Although
domestic violence is the most common form of violence
against women, it is distressing, too, to see all the different
types of violence that females experience, and the way it goes
on relentlessly throughout women's lives; the list in Box 8.2
is far from complete. According to the World Health Organization (WHO), rape is an ever-present threat and reality
for millions of women in developing countries.[1]

One thing comes across loud and clear; violence against

Box 8.1: Small glimpses of a big picture: figures on domestic violence[2]

◆ In every country where reliable large-scale studies have been conducted, between 10 per cent and 50 per cent of women report they have been physically abused by an intimate partner in their lifetime.[3]

◆ In 1996, it was found that one in every six women in Cambodia had experienced domestic violence, and more than seven in ten knew a family where violence was common.[4]

◆ A 1995 study in the city of León, Nicaragua, found that 60 per cent of women interviewed had been the victims of physical, sexual or psychological violence. Thirty-one per cent of abused women suffered physical violence during pregnancy.[5]

◆ In Rio de Janeiro, 25 per cent of men interviewed by researchers said they had used physical violence at least once against an intimate female partner.[6]

◆ A survey of Ugandan women of child-bearing age found that 30 per cent of them had experienced threats or physical abuse from their current partner, 20 per cent of them in the year preceding the interview.[7]

women is not something out of the ordinary. It appears to be endemic in all societies, whether affluent or poor, although there are variations both in terms of prevalence and public attitudes. There is some good news, though. The rights dimensions are now well recognised by the human rights movement, thanks to tireless women's activism throughout the last few decades. This was signalled in 2004, if not before, when Amnesty International launched its 'Stop Violence against Women' campaign. In its press release, Amnesty branded the issue a 'human rights atrocity', and laid responsibility on governments, local authorities,

Box 8.2: Violence against women through the life-cycle

◆ abortion of female foetuses
◆ female infanticide and neglect
◆ female genital mutilation
◆ rape
◆ sexual assault
◆ coercive sex
◆ trafficking
◆ sexual harassment
◆ domestic violence
◆ dowry abuse and murders
◆ widow inheritance and 'ritual cleansing'
◆ abuse of the elderly.

religious, business and community leaders to act against it.[8] There is a large, although loosely organised, movement of grass-roots women's organisations opposing violence against women worldwide, and agencies such as Oxfam support some of them, recognising that it is a major development issue.

Paying the costs of rights abuse

The UN has defined violence against women quite broadly, as 'any act of gender-based violence that results in, or is likely to result in, physical, sexual or psychological harm or suffering to women, including threats of such acts, coercion or arbitrary deprivation of liberty, whether occurring in public or private life'.[9] The term covers violence that is inflicted on a woman *because* she is a woman, such as female genital mutilation, and violence that affects women *disproportionately*, such as rape.

Women's right to be free from violence is an enabling right, like the rights to political participation and education.

According to the United Nations Emergency Fund for Children (UNICEF), violence against women is 'one of the most pervasive of human rights violations, denying women and girls equality, security, dignity, self-worth, and their right to enjoy fundamental freedoms'.[10] It also entails massive costs that are rarely acknowledged. For instance, it is a big contributory factor in the HIV/AIDS epidemic that is deepening poverty across sub-Saharan Africa (see Chapter 9). That is just one example of its pernicious public health and development impacts. According to the World Bank, health problems arising from rape and violence against women account for 5 per cent of global disease,[11] and the WHO views it as 'an urgent public health issue worldwide'.[12]

Health consequences include physical injury, depression, attempted suicide, chronic pain, psychosomatic disorders and a variety of reproductive health problems. Only a few attempts have been made to quantify the costs to society of treating these. As well as medical costs, there are the costs of police, social workers, counsellors, refuges and so on. So far, most attempts have focused on domestic violence and have been mainly confined to rich countries such as the United States, New Zealand, and Canada, although there have also been some studies in Latin America. Although it may seem heartless, counting the public costs can make governments sit up and take notice. For instance, in 1996, it was estimated that 'intimate partner violence' cost the London Borough of Hackney in the UK £7.5 million, or around $11 million. The mayor of Greater London, Ken Livingstone, estimates that domestic violence costs the city £278 million a year (around $417 million).[13] Of course, direct costs are only an issue where services exist. Many poor women who suffer abuse in the global South have no access to services of any kind.

As well as the obvious costs, there are heavy indirect ones, too. Women who are less productive because of domestic violence earn lower incomes, and these lower incomes in turn lead to lower economic demand. In Bangladesh, a poor rural woman may be beaten by her husband for 'dishonouring the family' by going to the market to sell chickens or getting a job processing rice; in these situations, domestic violence and sexual harassment deter women from getting involved in productive activities. Many women workers in the global South also face routine sexual harassment at work, which may deter women from looking for a job; see Box 8.3. Indirect socio-economic costs like these are almost impossible to quantify.

And what are the impacts on human development? Amartya Sen has pointed out that women in the global South, when allowed to be, are important agents of change, promoting social transformations that can alter everyone's lives, not only their own. As examples, he partly attributes two very positive South Asian trends, falling fertility rates and improved child survival rates, to women's increased ability to make decisions for themselves.[14] But constant vulnerability to violence, or the threat of it, undermines women's ability to make such decisions. Activists in Uttar Pradesh, India, acknowledged this when they commented at an Oxfam meeting that 'violence is not only a

Box 8.3: Sexual harassment at work

From Morocco to Honduras to Cambodia, interviewers researching the conditions of women factory workers for Oxfam's Make Trade Fair campaign heard many allegations of sexual harassment by male supervisors. One woman interviewed, Hasina, had been a garment worker in Bangalore, India, but decided that sex work was a preferable alternative: 'You are subjected to all kinds of sexual harassment in the factory. Supervisors, production managers and watchmen touch you without giving you anything in return. In this job, at least you are paid for the same.'[15]

violation of human rights but also deprives women from contributing to the development of the country, by affecting their confidence and self-esteem.'[16] Global issues such as chronic poverty, deforestation and public health problems cannot be solved without women's involvement, but violence bars many from contributing to their full potential.

Countering domestic and sexual violence

There are thousands of small women's organisations working on violence against women, and using the right to be free from violence as their reference point. Often they combine public education and lobbying activities with services such as counselling, legal advice and shelters. Two such organisations, Project Against Domestic Violence in Cambodia and Demus in Peru, are featured in Box 8.4. Across South Asia, Oxfam is working with hundreds of NGOs on the 'We Can' campaign, an imaginative response to the scale and severity of violence against women in that region; see the end of this chapter. There are also several men's initiatives aimed at reducing violence against women; see Box 8.5 for information about one of them, the White Ribbon Campaign. Another interesting example is Programme H, which works with young men in Brazil and Mexico, prompting them to question their attitudes to women and change their behaviour.[17]

Emergencies and conflicts

After disasters such as the 2004 tsunami, violence against women, both from their intimate partners and from other men, tends to increase. For instance, a recent survey found that at least six out of ten women in northern Uganda's largest camp for displaced people are sexually and physically assaulted, threatened and humiliated by men. The victims include girls as young as four. The surveyors found that only a tiny proportion of

Box 8.4: Women's organisations countering violence against women

The *Project against Domestic Violence* (PADV) is trying to get Cambodians to recognise domestic violence as a public issue rather than a private one. The organisation has produced a video, TV drama and the first Cambodian poster against domestic violence. PADV collaborated with two other organisations to put on a touring production about domestic violence. Using a traditional form of Cambodian theatre, the play branded domestic violence as a criminal act. Before each performance, PADV staff met local officials and community leaders to provide information on the law on domestic violence and the best ways to respond to it. This was a good way to involve them, because it gave them responsibility for addressing the issue. PADV workers also used the performances to give out information on the law and places to get help. The tour got a lot of media coverage. By stimulating public dialogue, PADV has managed to position domestic violence as a human rights issue, an important step forward.

Peruvian NGO *Demus* was set up in 1987 to focus on discrimination and violence against women, with an explicit focus on women's human rights rather than seeing those issues as an 'appendage of development'. The organisation has developed a three-pronged approach for working on the human rights of women who suffer from domestic and sexual violence: legal advice and representation, research and public education. An example of its public education work is its campaign 'Not one death more' (*Ni una muerta mas*). Staff monitor the national papers and record cases where women have been murdered by men. They have found that 20 per cent of the murdered women had been attacked by their murderers at least once previously, an indictment of the police's failure to respond.

The first stage is counselling, followed by legal advice where it is wanted. Demus has access both to established lawyers and a network of carefully selected law student volunteers. Involving the law students means free access to legal expertise, and there is the added bonus of creating a new generation of lawyers who are sensitive to the issues. When Demus helped the municipality of Miraflores to set up a help line there, it handled 1,200 cases in just three months. According to Maria Ysabel Cedano Garcia, the Demus network of volunteers is the key to its success. For instance, they helped to run one of the organisation's most influential campaigns, which publicised the case of Sandra Gonzales, from Lima. She was raped by local government officials, and when she reported the case to the police she was subjected to further sexual abuse. Demus' ensuing four-year campaign highlighted the need for changes in the justice system.

Box 8.5: 'Our strength is not for hurting'

The White Ribbon Campaign (WRC) to end violence against women started in 1991 in Canada, where it is now something of a national institution. It has also spread to over 30 other countries. The WRC aims to end men's silence about men's violence against women, raise awareness among men and boys and mobilise them to work for change through their schools, workplaces and communities. A look at WRC's Canadian website shows a poster of four tough-looking young men, under the slogan 'Our Strength is not for Hurting.'[18] According to founder Michael Kaufman,

WRC is based on the belief that, 'in most countries, the majority of men do not use physical or sexual violence; that we have been silent about that violence, and through the silence have allowed the violence to continue.'[19]

In most countries, activities start on 25th November, the International Day for the Elimination of Violence against Women, and continue until early December. Supporters wear a white ribbon as a public promise that they will never commit, condone or remain silent about violence against women. WRC staff, who are few in number, see themselves as catalysts, encouraging institutions such as schools, trade unions, companies, youth groups and NGOs to organise their own white ribbon activities. The tactic is to encourage men to take responsibility for ending violence against women, rather than laying blame on them. For instance, a poster which has been used in several countries has the headline 'These men want to put an end to violence against women,' followed by signatures of some prominent men. Remaining lines are left blank so that men and boys can sign the posters when they are put up at schools or workplaces.

Underlying the WRC's goal of ending the violence that many women endure is the wider aim of helping 'to end discrimination against women and girls, to achieve gender equality and equity, and to promote the human rights of women and girls'. For instance, a recent poster bears the words 'Have you ever noticed the WORST thing you can call a MAN is a WOMAN? What does that say about how we view women?'

attacks on women and girls were reported.[20] See the end of this chapter to find out about a creative initiative aimed at reducing domestic violence in Sri Lanka's post-tsunami camps.

Conflicts are another context in which violence against

women rises. Since the mass rape of women in Bosnia filled the headlines in the early 1990s, rape has been used to terrorise populations in several conflicts, for instance in Liberia, Sierra Leone, northern Uganda and Burundi, and at the time of writing, in the Darfur region of Sudan. Box 8.6 contains extracts from harrowing testimonies on rapes during the conflict in the Democratic Republic of Congo.

Box 8.6: Rape as a weapon of war in the Congo

When UN troops moved into the eastern part of the Democratic Republic of Congo in 2004, the scale and horrific nature of the rapes that had occurred there during six years of fighting started to emerge. In a war that went almost unnoticed by the world outside Africa, an estimated 3–4 million people were killed, and an estimated 40,000 women raped, although exact figures will never be known. Every one of the dozen or more warring militias ranging over the area used rape as a tactic to terrorise the civilian population. Troops from neighbouring countries that joined in the conflict have also been implicated. Experienced UN and international humanitarian NGO staff told Amnesty International researchers that they had never come across as many rape victims in a conflict situation as they had in the Congo. The rapes were characterised by extreme violence and brutality, with many victims suffering horrific injuries that need complex reconstructive surgery. There has also been a massive increase in sexually transmitted diseases, including syphilis, gonorrhoea and HIV/AIDS.

BBC reporter Jackie Martens interviewed one victim, 16-year-old Vumiliar Lukindo. In 2003 she endured a sadistic rape attack by two combatants, who murdered her unborn baby and inflicted terrible wounds on her. A year later she was still suffering severe pain and incontinence.[21] Another victim told Amnesty how rebels stopped a bus she was on in 2003. She and the five other women passengers were raped beside the road, then marched to the soldiers' camp. For two months, she was held there: 'For me, the most difficult [thing] was each time to be raped by so many different soldiers, every day.' Weak and injured, she at last managed to make her way home:

> My husband threw me out as soon as I got home. ... When I came out of the forest, when I reached the house, he decided to abandon me that same day. Now he has another wife. ... I ask myself, perhaps I have got AIDS. And I've deep pains here, in my lower stomach. I couldn't bear to sleep with a man now.[22]

Amnesty accused the DR Congo government of not doing enough either to provide medical services to the victims or to punish the rapists: 'The DR Congo government must assume its responsibility to prevent, punish and eradicate sexual violence, and demonstrate that such behaviour is not tolerated.'[23]

Breakthroughs

Getting violence against women officially recognised as a human rights violation has been a great achievement for activists. Inexplicably, CEDAW itself had failed to mention the issue directly, but that was partially rectified in 1992, when the CEDAW Committee issued a statement that said: 'gender-based violence is a form of discrimination that seriously inhibits women's ability to enjoy rights and freedoms on a basis of equality with men.'

The Committee also pointed out that States could be held responsible for private acts if they failed to prevent violations of rights, or to investigate and punish acts of violence.[24] Amnesty International argues that repeated domestic violence falls within the ambit of the Convention against Torture and Other Cruel, Inhuman or Degrading Treatment or Punishment, and should be dealt with as such.

As far as violence against women during conflicts is concerned, the establishment of the International Criminal Court (ICC) in 1998 was a massive breakthrough. It came after years of intensive campaigning by women activists and in the teeth of stiff opposition from the US government, which at the time of writing is still trying its best to weaken it. The statute by which the ICC was established lists rape, sexual slavery, enforced prostitution, forced pregnancy, enforced sterilisation and other forms of sexual violence as war crimes and crimes against humanity. This is the first time international legislation has recognised crimes against women in this way. The ICC started its first formal investigation, into the crimes committed in the Democratic Republic of Congo, in 2004. Women's rights campaigners are keeping a careful eye on its proceedings, to monitor how effectively it investigates and punishes crimes against women.

We can end violence against women

Manisha Thakker was burned to death in mysterious circumstances in her home in Ahmedabad. Her parents were very suspicious, especially as none of the neighbours noticed any smoke or noise at the time of her death. 'Stove burnings' are a common cause of death among rural women in India, and murders are often disguised like this. They reported their suspicions to the police, who at first refused to even register an initial report. However, with the help of NGO Jyoti Sangh, they got the police to draw up an official report. Manisha's husband, Brijesh, had been demanding 30,000 rupees to buy a new bike, and had told her to get the money from her parents. When she refused, he repeatedly beat her, and he and his family denied her food. Following Manisha's death, Brijesh and his parents were arrested, although they managed to obtain bail. On Jyoti Sangh's advice, Manisha's parents then took the case to a higher court, whereupon they were re-arrested and tried.[25]

Stories like Manisha Thakker's are common in Indian newspapers, but they are only the tip of the iceberg. In South Asia, one in two women faces violence in her daily life. It starts before birth. There are 50 million fewer women in South Asia today than there should be, because of sex-selective abortions, as well as female infanticide and the neglect of girl children.

Once past infancy, many Indian girls and women have to endure daily beatings, and an estimated 15,000 are murdered each year in crimes linked to dowry extortion; this despite the fact that dowry has been illegal for 40 years. In the city of Bangalore alone, there are an estimated six 'dowry deaths' every day.[26] In Bangladesh, 47 per cent of women suffer domestic violence, and the country has its own ghastly form of violence against women: acid burnings. In Pakistan, the Interior Minister recently admitted that 2,774 women have been murdered in so-called 'honour killings' in the past five years, although many activists think this an underestimate. Meanwhile, an estimated 5–7,000 young Nepalese women are trafficked across the borders every year, most ending up in Indian brothels.

In response, Oxfam has helped to start the We Can campaign to end violence against women, which now involves 400 different organisations across South Asia. From the start, the campaigners realised that they had to tackle deeply entrenched attitudes, ultimately stemming from a belief that women are worth less than men. The campaign, projected to run until 2011, focuses on domestic violence in Bangladesh, Sri Lanka, Nepal and India, and so-called 'honour killings' in Pakistan.

Thousands of posters, pamphlets, post cards, hoardings, murals, T-shirts, bookmarks and screensavers feature the campaign strap-line, 'Equal relationships are violence free', while theatre, puppet shows, cultural festivals, boat races, rallies, door-knocking campaigns and protest marches all help to spread the word. In India, the campaign was launched with a two-day festival that brought together 800 students from different parts of the country. In Nepal, 30 victims of trafficking told their chilling stories to a shocked audience attending a 'Woman's Court'.

We Can has an unusual and ambitious strategy, which is to mobilise 5 million 'change makers' across the region. Shamim Ara Begum, Executive Director of Polli Sree, explains:

> A change maker is any ordinary man or woman who speaks up, breaks the silence and acts to stop violence against women. They do not have to be heroes, but they have to be open-minded and willing to take a stand. Through these people, change will happen slowly but surely, like ripples in the water.

Their role is to get a further 50 million people to take a visible stand against violence against women, bringing about a fundamental shift in public attitudes.

Change maker Santosh Pandey mobilised fellow students to speak out against the sexual harassment that dogged the lives of female students at his college in Varanasi. The situation was so threatening that many were afraid to go the library or the common room, and some abandoned their studies altogether. The college administration, although aware of the problem, had done little about it. Motivated chiefly by Santosh, a group of concerned students forced the administration to act. They also set up a students' union, to which a young woman from a so-called 'backward community' was elected as an officer. This was enough to earn Santosh enemies among the more privileged students, and in 2003 he and his wife were deliberately run down. She lost the baby she was carrying, and Santosh was seriously injured. Although this has been a severe blow to the students' union, the other students still look to him as a mentor and guide.

Another Indian change maker involved in the campaign is 40-year-old Kulsum Bibi in Orissa. After suffering domestic violence herself, she realised that most women in her village were regularly beaten, and that few had any way out. When a woman raped by her husband's relatives sought her help, Kulsum asked the village council to intervene. The council ordered the husband's family to pay the rape victim compensation, which meant she could leave her husband's home and start a small business to support herself. This small victory was the start of Kulsum's crusade against domestic violence. She now provides individual advice and counselling, and runs monthly self-help and support meetings for local women. One of the worst cases she has had to act on was a brutal dowry murder. It was Kulsum who reported the death to the police and, with the help of other local activists, organised protests against the husband. He absconded and, though caught later, was released on bail. Kulsum and her supporters are determined to get him punished for his crime, something that, sadly, cannot be taken for granted in rural India.[27]

In Sri Lanka, water tanks in tsunami camps are doubling as We Can hoardings. Scenes of domestic violence have been painted on their sides, along with messages like 'Violence destroys the whole family.' More women than men died in the tsunami, and women survivors face increased domestic violence. Shanthi Sivanesan, an Oxfam staff member working on the tsunami-affected eastern coast of Sri Lanka, explains:

From the very beginning we heard about harassment and abuse against women in the camps – mostly within families. ... Sometimes we could even hear fighting and beating from within tents as we walked through camps. We knew that somehow we had to get the message of stopping violence against women through – all the way to the community. Suddenly we had the idea of painting the messages on water tanks. The tanks make perfect canvases – and they are gathering places so lots of people would see the messages. It has been really successful. People stand around the tanks discussing the images and slogans. Other camp leaders have come to us asking for the same for their water tanks.

Since then, Oxfam has painted tanks in other camps.[28]

9
Women's rights abuses help to spread HIV/AIDS

Over 62 per cent of people living with HIV are in sub-Saharan Africa, where young women (aged 15 to 24) are the worst-affected group. There is a strong connection between women's rights abuses and the virus's rapid spread in the region. Young women's lack of social and economic power, and their routine exposure to violence, increase their vulnerability to infection. In general, women also suffer the social impacts of the epidemic more than men, for instance because the task of looking after sick family members and AIDS orphans usually falls to them. Women need cheap methods for protecting themselves against infection and policy measures that tackle the roots of their vulnerability, such as strengthening the criminal justice system to deal with violence against women and changing the law so that women can inherit land and property.

> VAW and HIV/AIDS are dual epidemics overlapping in women's lives.
> Centre for the Study of Violence and
> Reconciliation, South Africa[1]

HIV/AIDS is the largest epidemic in human history; nothing like it has been seen before. In the words of Botswana's President Festus Mogae, 'The HIV/AIDS pandemic is the most serious global challenge facing humanity at the present time. ... It poses a threat to global security, peace as well as sustained development.'[2] Globally, women account for 45 per cent of people infected with HIV, but that figure hides big differences between regions. No other part of the world comes close to sub-Saharan Africa's high prevalence levels; the region has just over 10 per cent of the world's population, but is home to 63 per cent of all people living with HIV. Nor does any other region show such a disproportionate impact on women and girls (see Box 9.1). For these reasons, and because HIV/AIDS in sub-Saharan Africa is closely bound up with women's human rights abuses, I focus on that region here.

Of course, HIV is an increasing threat to other parts of the world too. If current trends continue, Asia might soon become the new centre of the epidemic, with both India and China facing potential catastrophes. In 2005, the Joint United Nations Programme on HIV/AIDS (UNAIDS) reported steep increases in HIV infections in Central and East Asia, and by 2006 there were over 8.5 million people living with HIV in Asia.[3] Although there were success stories in the 1990s, when both Cambodia and Thailand succeeded in curbing their epidemics, in Asia as a whole there are signs that it has spread from high-risk groups (mainly injecting drug users and sex workers) into the general population. In sub-Saharan Africa, on the other hand, heterosexual sex is the main transmission mode for HIV, which partly explains why the epidemic there is impacting on women so disastrously.

Box 9.1: Figures on HIV/AIDS[4]

◆ Estimated number of adults living with HIV worldwide: 37.2 million.

◆ Proportion of infected adults worldwide who are women: 47 per cent.

◆ Proportion of infected adults in sub-Saharan Africa who are women: 62 per cent.

◆ In sub-Saharan Africa, three out of four 15–24 year olds living with HIV are female.

Rights abuses create vulnerability for women

What explains the huge disparity between men and women's HIV infection rates in sub-Saharan Africa, especially for people 15–24 years old? Physiologically, women are twice as likely as men to contract HIV through an act of heterosexual sex. But there is more to it than this; the rapid spread of HIV/AIDS in the region is also tied up with the denial of women's human rights, including endemic violence against women. When women live with violence as an ever-present threat, it is hard for them to protect themselves from HIV infection. As a case in point, South Africa has become notorious for its high levels of violence against women, and also has the highest prevalence of HIV/AIDS in the world. Is this entirely a coincidence? There are many other, less obvious rights denials that combine to weaken women's bargaining power in sexual relationships and so contribute to the epidemic; Box 9.2 lists some of these. Official responses have not addressed these connections, with the result that HIV/AIDS has swept through populations with bewildering speed.

As well as straightforward sexual violence, the so-called 'sugar-daddy' scenario also exposes young African women to terrible risk. An estimated 12 million children in sub-Saharan Africa have lost one or both parents to AIDS, and about half of these are girls.[5] Apart from female AIDS orphans, there are millions of other young girls trapped in poverty and with no opportunities. Little wonder that girls and young women in southern and eastern Africa often get involved in sexual relationships with older men in exchange for food, money, presents or some other form of help. In Box 9.3, Monique Wanjala explains the kind of situation that young Kenyan girls can find themselves in, and Angeline Mugwendere of CAMA spells out the connections between poverty, school fees, sugar daddies and HIV/AIDS.

While young, unmarried women are vulnerable, being married and faithful to one's husband offers no protection, either.

Box 9.2: Women's human rights issues linked to HIV/AIDS in sub-Saharan Africa

- Violence against women limits their ability to say 'no' to unwanted sex, so increases their risk of becoming infected.

- Property and inheritance laws tend to discriminate against women and leave them economically dependent on men, and AIDS widows may be stripped of their land.

- Discriminatory divorce laws make it harder for wives to leave abusive husbands, even if they know they are infected with HIV.

- Widows may be forced to undergo traditional practices such as 'wife inheritance' that heighten their risk.

- Poverty propels girls into 'sugar-daddy' scenarios where they exchange sexual favours for gifts of cash.

- Girls' early marriage usually means their husbands are older than they are. It puts girls at risk of infection, because older husbands are more likely to be infected and the age difference means wives are likely to have less power in the relationship.

- Girls and women are less likely than boys and men to know how to protect themselves against infection, partly because of their lower educational levels.

- Girls' education is an important weapon in fighting the spread of AIDS, but there are still gender gaps when it comes to enrolling in and attending school.

- Female-controlled prevention methods, such as the female condom and microbicides, are not yet widely available.

- Women's lack of resources and low social status usually means they are less likely to get medical treatment and care than men.

In fact, research in Kenya and Zambia has found that young married women are at a higher risk of HIV infection than their unmarried counterparts.[6] In a study in Zambia, only 11 per cent of women interviewed thought they had the right to ask their husbands to use condoms, even if they knew the men were unfaithful and HIV-positive.[7] The story of Ugandan woman Sules K, interviewed by Human Rights Watch (Box 9.4), seems to be far from unusual. If you know refusing to have sex or asking your partner to wear a condom is likely to result in a beating, being assertive is not a viable option. According to a recent study of women in Soweto, South Africa, women who were beaten by their husbands or boyfriends were 48 per cent more likely to become infected by HIV than those who were not.[8]

Why do so many women like Sules K put up with abuse like

Box 9.3: The bitter truth about sugar daddies

'Generally [girls and young women] lack the social and economic empowerment to make choices that will protect them against HIV infection. The biggest challenge a young woman faces is her inability to negotiate safe sex by choosing the terms upon which she will have sex with a particular partner. Many adolescent girls have their first sexual encounter with much older men and this first experience often involves an amount of force, causing cuts and tears to the vagina, increasing the risk of HIV infection. Young women frequently remain in high-risk relationships due to economic dependence on their partners. Their access to the right information on HIV/AIDS is also limited and there is much misinformation.'

Monique Wanjala, a young woman living
with HIV and a member of
Women Fighting AIDS in Kenya[9]

'My fees were paid by an NGO, but I had to watch with pain in my heart as my friends got desperate to find ways to stay in school. Like me, they wanted to be recognised because of their education, and knew that schooling was the only way out of poverty for them. So they took the shortest possible way to achieve that, dangerous as it was. They went on to sleep with sugar daddies in return for cash to pay their fees. And many of them contracted AIDS. With access to school, these girls would be alive today and would have had a chance to make something out of their lives, as I have. We can break this vicious cycle of poverty, by abolishing fees and supporting girls through school. World leaders should do everything it takes to keep girls in school – whatever the cost, it's worth it.'

Angeline Mugwendere, 24,
CAMA, Zimbabwe[10]

this? One underlying reason is the widespread discrimination against women when it comes to owning land and other property (see Chapter 6). Denied property rights, and with less chance than men of getting a decent education and then a decent job, millions of women are trapped in dependency, with their bargaining power in relationships severely limited.

Once a woman has become infected with HIV in sub-Saharan Africa, she has less chance of getting access to treatment and care than a man. In southern Africa, for instance, only a tiny proportion of AIDS-infected people are receiving drug treatment, and most of them are educated urban men. In Zambia, more men than women came forward for HIV treatment even after the government drastically reduced the price, and this in a country where women make up well over half of people living with HIV. The reasons HIV-positive women gave for not seeking

Box 9.4: Marriage may be no protection

'My husband would beat me to the point that he was too ashamed to take me to the doctor. He forced me to have sex with him and beat me if I refused. ... Even when he was HIV-positive he still wanted sex. He refused to use a condom. He said he cannot eat sweets with the paper on.'

Sules K, widow, Uganda[11]

treatment included poverty and the fact that, where money was limited, families generally decided to pay for drugs for male family members rather than girls and women.[12] Botswana, on the other hand, has an exemplary programme, with HIV treatment available to anyone who needs it; here, the ratio of women and men receiving treatment is 3:2.[13]

What happens when a woman becomes an AIDS widow? In the decades to come, this will happen to millions of women in the region. Like Margaret Atieno (Box 9.5), many will be subjected to the harrowing experience of being driven off their property by male relatives of their deceased husbands. In addition, women who are widowed, regardless of the cause of the husband's death, commonly undergo traditional practices such

Box 9.5: Widows lack property rights

'When my husband died I was chased from my home by my husband's cousin. ... He came with a club and chased me, running. He said, "A woman that has been bought by cattle can't stay in his homestead." He said I should go away so that he could till the land. If I had had a son, he wouldn't have chased me out of the homestead.'

Margaret Atieno,
Siaya, western Kenya[14]

as wife inheritance or 'sexual cleansing'. Wife inheritance is the term used when a widow has sex with her dead husband's brother; it is believed to dispel evil forces, and the brother-in-law is then free to take over the dead man's property, including his widow. Emily Owino's story in Box 9.6 shows what 'sexual cleansing' means. It hardly needs saying that, especially where AIDS has caused the husband's death, practices like these fuel the HIV epidemic, creating a vicious circle of infection. Where they happen against the woman's will, as in Mrs Owino's case, they are also rights violations in themselves.

Looking after sick people and children is traditionally 'women's work'; so the caring burden of HIV/AIDS falls heavily on females of all ages. At one end of the life-cycle, it starts with young girls; they are more likely than boys to be withdrawn from school, or not enrolled at all, when AIDS strikes a family. They find themselves becoming carers, doing the housework and/or bringing money into the home through domestic service,

Box 9.6: The practice of 'sexual cleansing'

Shortly after Emily Owino's husband died, her in-laws took all her possessions – including farm equipment, live-stock, household goods and clothing. The in-laws insisted that she be 'cleansed' by having sex with a herdsman, a social outcast, as a condition for staying in her home. They paid the man to have sex with Mrs Owino, against her will and without a condom; later they took over her farmland. She sought help from the local elder and chief, who did nothing, and her in-laws forced her out of her home. She and her children were homeless until someone offered her a small, leaky shack. As she could no longer afford their school fees, her children dropped out of school.

Based on an interview with Emily Owino,
Siaya, western Kenya[15]

street-trading, gifts from 'sugar daddies' or undisguised sex work. Research in Zimbabwe found that 76 per cent of children dropping out of school to look after sick relatives were girls.[16] At the other end of the life-cycle, millions of grandmothers are looking after their orphaned grandchildren at a time of life when they hoped they would have a rest from drudgery.

Ways forward

At the practical level, women urgently need methods for avoiding infection during sex, so that their health and survival no longer depends on persuading their partners to 'eat a sweet with the wrapper on'. The female condom is in high demand in countries where it is being actively promoted, such as South Africa, Ghana and Zimbabwe, but it is expensive and has other drawbacks. For one thing, it prevents conception as well as infection, so it is unsuitable for women who want children. Microbicides that can prevent the sexual transmission of HIV and other diseases are now being tested. They come in various forms, including gels and suppositories. Because they are undetectable and can be applied several hours before sex, they do not need cooperation from male partners, so they could enable women to take control of their own protection.

Microbicides could make a big impact on the rate of HIV transmission, but only if research and development investment is increased dramatically. The trouble is, there is not enough money-making potential to get pharmaceutical companies interested. In the words of Ilene Wong, a doctor who has worked on AIDS in Africa: 'pharmaceutical companies would be more persistent in their efforts if the main beneficiaries of microbicides were not impoverished African women'.[17] That means funding has to come from governments and charities, but it is not flowing in sufficient quantities. Given microbicides' potential, it is hard to understand the aid donors' niggardliness, especially when USAID is spending large sums on the much-criticised 'ABC' strategy. ABC stands for Abstinence, Being Faithful and Using Condoms, but it misses the point that many African women have little choice in these matters. The Global Campaign for Microbicides is calling for public funding for research and development to be increased, so that microbicides become available without unnecessary delay.[18]

Young women, especially, need information about HIV/AIDS. Generally, women in sub-Saharan Africa are less well informed about HIV than are men. In particular, data from 35 of the 48 countries in sub-Saharan Africa shows that, on average, young men are 20 per cent more likely to have correct knowledge of HIV than young women.[19] Women also need policy changes that attack the social and economic roots of their vulnerability. A good place to start would be improving criminal justice systems, so that violence against women is punished. In some countries, this means putting new legislation on the statute books, because, according to Human Rights Watch, several countries in the region have no laws specifically relating to domestic violence.[20] Training police officers and judges to take violence against women seriously is another useful strategy, and the Ugandan government's experience of establishing family protection units could be learned from in other countries. Public information campaigns to raise awareness that domestic violence is a criminal act are also effective; as well as changing attitudes, they encourage women to bring cases to the police.

If more women in sub-Saharan Africa could afford to leave abusive marriages, fewer would contract HIV/AIDS. But the dice are loaded against them. Throughout Africa, male-dominated governments have ignored their CEDAW commitments to do something about customary laws that discriminate against women, such as land inheritance rules. As Dorcas Coker-Appiah of Ghana's Gender Studies and Human Rights Centre has pointed out, it is not in their interests to do so.[21] Nothing daunted, campaigners hope that the provisions of the Protocol to the African Charter on Human and Peoples' Rights on the

Box 9.7: Girls' education is a weapon against HIV/AIDS

◆ Literate women are four times more likely than illiterate women to know the main ways to avoid AIDS.[22]

◆ Young women in Rwanda with secondary or higher education are five times as likely to know the main HIV transmission routes than young women who had no formal education.[23]

◆ Better-educated girls delay sexual activity until later in life and are more likely to expect their partners to use condoms.[24]

Rights of Women, mentioned in Chapter 2, will address this as governments start to incorporate it into domestic law.

Another rights issue at the heart of the African HIV epidemic is girls' poor access to good-quality education (see Box 9.7). Educating girls, especially getting more of them through secondary school, is one of the best ways to lower infection rates among young women. It is not just a matter of having the knowledge to protect themselves from infection, although this is important. Educated girls are also more confident and have a higher status than young women who have never been to school, so they are in a better position to decide who to have sex with and whether or not to use a condom. During the 1990s, when there was a decline in HIV prevalence among women in Zambia, the greatest reductions were found among well-educated women, while prevalence among the least educated either remained stable or increased.[25] The trouble is, African secondary schools themselves are too often sites of abuse; see Chapter 7. This can be addressed by developing policies on sexual harassment at school and vigorously enforcing them, while modules on HIV/AIDS and violence against women need to be taught in life-skills courses. There are plenty of examples of good work along these lines, but the overall picture on girls' education is ominous. In 2004, the GCE claimed that failure to provide all the world's children with a complete primary education would result in 700,000 cases of HIV in young adults every year, cases that would otherwise have been prevented.[26]

In the 1990s, Thailand showed that HIV prevalence levels can be reduced by determined and strategic efforts involving government, civil society and businesses. The challenge is much greater in sub-Saharan Africa; resources are fewer and the epidemic is more generalised than it had been in Thailand. Nonetheless, at least one African country, Uganda has managed to substantially reduce HIV prevalence since the early 1990s, showing that it can be done; strong political will and leadership seem to have been important ingredients in this success.[27] As an illustration of a successful community-based initiative with a strong rights focus, the story below documents a project aimed at empowering girls and young women in Zambia.

Girls are not groundnuts

The Zambian government has good policies on women's rights in relation to HIV/AIDS and health, and has ratified both the CRC and CEDAW. Despite these policies, poverty, gender inequality and outdated cultural norms are giving rise to high rates of unwanted early pregnancy, sexually transmitted infections and HIV and AIDS. At the end of 2005, an estimated 17 per cent of Zambians aged 15–49 years old were living with HIV or AIDS, 57 per cent of them females. The HIV prevalence among females aged 14–19 years is six times that of males in the same age group.[28]

In this context, the International HIV/AIDS Alliance has been working with the Planned Parenthood Association of Zambia, ministries and communities in the Eastern Province to realise sexual and reproductive rights for young women and men and support responsible sexual behaviour.

Initial discussions with community elders, teachers, health practitioners and young men and women themselves highlighted a range of challenges. Poverty was quickly identified as a major part of the problem. People have few choices for survival and are often forced to use dangerous or objectionable coping strategies which they would not turn to if they were better off. In some poor households girls are pressurised to support the family by selling sex or by marrying against their will.

Men's attitudes were also critiqued. Many older men believe that they are entitled to have sex with dependent girls, with or without their consent, in the same way that they might 'eat a groundnut from their farm'. Husbands also believe they are entitled to sex with their wives at any time, and to have sex outside marriage. For their part, girls are taught at puberty to acquiesce to men's sexual demands. All this runs counter to Zambian legislation and government policies on women's rights.

As part of the programme, girls and boys now discuss these issues at school. They read stories about how their peers have resisted unwanted sexual proposals, reported abuse and sought help from trusted older people. They practise assertiveness skills and talk about how they would like to treat each other with respect, equality and care. Drama is a popular activity. For instance, one group has developed a play about the practice of older men marrying young girls so they can acquire cows through the dowry. It is usually followed by a discussion exploring how households can manage their resources in such a way as to protect the rights of all family members. Meanwhile, girls are learning that they have a legal right to refuse to marry or sell sex. They look for adults in their community who will support them, should they find themselves in situations like these.

Traditional initiation advisors, *alangizi*, play an important role in girls' lives around puberty, teaching girls how to perform sexually. The traditional ways do nothing to protect girls from unwanted pregnancies, sexually transmitted infections and HIV and AIDS. The programme has helped many *alangizi* to reflect on what they are teaching, and many no longer teach girls how to perform sexually as soon as they start to menstruate. The public display of scantily-dressed girls dancing for the assembled village, to demonstrate what they have learned, is also becoming less common. Girls reaching puberty are taught they have a right to refuse sex and encouraged to make safe choices like using condoms. These community activities are reinforced by radio programmes. Young people write in to 'Radio Breeze' with their problems, which are discussed on air. The broadcasts are helping to create a culture of rights which both young people and adults can buy into.

Already people have noticed changes. Girls feel they can act assertively and get help to uphold their rights, and boys are more likely to support them than in the past. Meanwhile, the older generation is talking about how their culture needs to adapt. People report that teenage pregnancies, the number of girls leaving school early and sexually transmitted infections are all decreasing. Girls have started to blow the whistle on sexual harassment and abuse, rather than accepting it. As one said:

> We now know what our rights are and we are asking for them. I didn't know that an older man is not allowed to propose me for sex – I thought that I have to respect him and give him what he asks for. Now I know that I am not just a 'groundnut' to be eaten whenever he feels like it, I am a human being with rights.

Not everyone was happy with the programme at first, though. A local chief initially objected to the Radio Breeze programmes: 'This radio programme should stop; why are you trying to attack our culture? Young girls are refusing to have sex with me. This is unheard of!' But after journalists from the channel met him to explain what they were doing, he threw his influence behind the programme's objectives, bringing his headmen with him.

So far, all the indications are that the programme itself is a success, but the wider picture still gives concern. Changes in the donor environment are making it more difficult to promote young people's sexual and reproductive rights. For instance, the US government, a major funder, is now pushing sexual abstinence as the way forward, and this is making condoms less acceptable or available for young people. It is a short-sighted policy, driven by the US religious right rather than objective assessments of what works and what does not, and it threatens a decade of gains for women. However, young Zambians are demanding their rights to information and services, and the project will support them in this.

Meanwhile, poverty in Zambia continues to get worse, undermining sexual and reproductive health and contributing to girls' and women's vulnerability. For many girls, finding an older man to pay school fees or lend money is the only way to climb out of the poverty trap. As long as they and their communities cannot exercise their economic rights, for instance the right to a fair price for their labour and produce, young women's sexual and reproductive rights are also denied. Recognising these connections, project staff and volunteers plan to work more closely with economic programmes supporting young women, as well as lobbying for fair trade and debt relief.

(Adapted from an article by Gill Gordon,
International HIV/AIDS Alliance)

10
The future is already happening

There are two phenomena looming over us that will have far-reaching effects on women's human rights in the next 10–20 years, and which I have not yet mentioned. They are: new technologies being developed at bewildering speed, and climate change due to greenhouse gas emissions, which is already wreaking havoc on women's lives in some parts of the global South. To find out how we might expect them to impact on women's rights, especially in the global South, I spoke to two specialists in these fields: Ann Elisabeth Samson of the Association for Women's Rights in Development, and Ulrike Röhr of Genanet, a German organisation working for gender justice in environmental and sustainability policy.

New technologies: Ann Elisabeth Samson

G.T.   Can you define what is covered by the phrase 'new technologies', and their significance for women's human rights?

A.E.S.   What particularly interests me as a feminist are developments in reproductive technologies, biotechnology involving humans, animals and plants, information and communication technology, military hardware and nanotechnology. They all have the potential to make fundamental changes, both good and bad, to our bodies, our environments, our work and our safety. They all have ramifications that could affect women's ability to exercise their human rights in one way or another, but reproductive and genetic technologies are usually thought of as being the most relevant to women.

The tough thing about looking at new technologies in relation to women's rights is that there is such a wide range of impacts technologies can have. Many have the potential to improve women's lives, like some of the information and communication technologies among others, while others are more insidious, and still others can be directly harmful. But one thing remains constant: they are being developed and used in a context of unequal power relations between men and women, and their development and use has not usually focused on women's needs, or on women's health and rights.

G.T. Can you give an example of how these new technologies affect women?

A.E.S. For instance, genetic modification of plants is particularly important to women farmers in the global South. They are doing most of the work to feed their families and communities through their subsistence farming, and it is often women who pass on indigenous knowledge about agriculture, local foods and medicines, yet they have no 'voice' when it comes to influencing what is developed or how it is disseminated. When market forces are combined with GM plants that can be grown in more places, women lose their plots of land to cash crops, often controlled by men. And we have some evidence that when a new technological input for agriculture is introduced, women tend to be pushed out of the primary roles of using that technology.

If we look at biotechnology in general, much of it is being 'sold' to us as a way of improving health and extending our lives. But it's important to keep in mind just who are the targets for these new medicines and other advances. They are geared towards rich society's problems, such as erectile dysfunction, for which Viagra was developed, heart disease, diabetes and other problems of the developed world, while they largely ignore the problems of the poor. Specifically with regards to women's rights, what isn't considered is how women's roles are affected by these changes; increased life expectancy, for instance. Because women tend to be the caregivers of the sick and elderly, they are disproportionately affected. Of course, the kinds of technologies most often associated with women's rights are related to reproduction.

G.T.   You mentioned that reproductive technologies were particularly relevant. Can you say a bit more about this?

A.E.S. The phrase 'reproductive technologies' covers devices and procedures for assisting, preventing or manipulating contraception and fertility, influencing how we have children and influencing children's characteristics. New reproductive technologies, or NRTs for short, are increasingly effective. They are being developed and marketed through a globalised system of profit seeking and control, giving rise to ethical concerns about the commodification of human life and the marketing of women's bodies. NRTs such as pre-implantation genetic diagnosis, cloning and even IVF are starting to redefine how human life is created, as well as who and what can be reproduced. Not only can an embryo now be created outside the body, but the 'artificial womb', which although it doesn't exist yet is already in development, would enable an embryo to be brought to term outside a body too. Women are particularly affected by NRTs because of their reproductive role, and because they have to be tested on women and their genetic material.

G.T.   I think a lot of people would be surprised to hear you argue that reproductive technologies may threaten women's human rights, when they enable women to control their fertility. Don't technologies such as IVF actually enhance women's rights?

A.E.S.   There are two big issues here. First, it is true that new reproductive technologies give women some control, but they are not necessarily the appropriate technology for women's needs. Look at the contraceptive pill. Many women around the world use it, but it provides no protection against sexually transmitted infections like HIV, and it means women have to take daily doses of hormones that might harm them in the long term.

There is the potential for misuse too. Take ultrasound; it is said that these days, even the most remote Indian village has access to an ultrasound machine. It can make birth and pregnancy much safer for women, but it is being used to discover the sex of a foetus and enable sex-selective abortions, to the extent that women in these areas are becoming an 'endangered species'. The new technique of genetic diagnosis before the egg has been implanted in the uterus makes sex selection even easier, because intervention can happen before conception. It is already being marketed in some wealthier parts of the world. As more NRTs are developed, including next-generation assisted fertility technologies and the contraceptive vaccine, women have to keep asking questions about whether or not they are the most appropriate technologies for them.

The other main point I want to make is that we have to do some serious thinking about what is a right and what isn't. Women's right to control their fertility is very different from the so-called 'right' to have a baby at whatever age you want or choose what colour eyes your baby is going to have, for instance. Companies who promote NRTs use rights language, and this can be confusing. Feminists might hesitate to call for regulation for fear that bans will limit women's choice.

Finally, I think it's really important to take note of the way these new technologies are globalised. For example, I was searching on Amazon.com for a book about infertility recently and two advertisements popped up, one for an IVF clinic in Turkey and another in Argentina, advertising cheap IVF services in their clinics. This kind of thing has been called 'medical tourism'. Not only are there concerns for women's safety in using these clinics, but they've prompted a new set of questions. There have been situations in the last 20 years or so where women in the South were used to test reproductive technologies that were then marketed to women in the North. The development and dissemination of these new technologies is truly global and not just relevant for the wealthy women who can afford them.

G.T.   So what do you think is the way forward?

A.E.S.   The development and dissemination of new technologies should be subject to the same democratic standards as any other global process. Decisions should be openly debated and open to public scrutiny; they cannot be left to individual businessmen and scientists. We need to slow down and ask more questions about which, how and why technologies are developed, rather than just react to breakthroughs as they are made. For instance, if women could direct contraceptive technology, what would it look like? Would it be different from the methods we have now? We need to find and encourage technologies that improve the quality of life and help secure human rights for everyone.

Young women are particularly important here; in general, younger people tend to adopt new technologies more quickly than the older generation, and by the same token, young women are far more adept at navigating new technologies, especially for their benefit.

Climate change: Ulrike Röhr

G.T.   Many of us have noticed changes in our climate, and increasingly the news carries stories about the melting Arctic ice-cap and other alarming climatic phenomena. What is happening to our climate and what will be the results?

U.R.   Put simply, in the next hundred years, the world is expected to carry on warming up by between 1.4 and 5.8°C, and sea levels are predicted to rise by between 0.09 and 0.88 metres. Apart from George Bush's tame scientists, the world's scientific community generally accepts that these changes are mainly due to emissions of greenhouse gases caused by the burning of fossil fuels. As well as gradual climatic changes, we can expect more extreme climate events, and worse ones. For instance, Hurricane Katrina, that caused the catastrophic flooding of New Orleans, was very violent, and a top climate-change expert in the UK said that was due to a rise in sea temperatures caused by global warming. The frequency of super-violent hurricanes like Katrina and Wilma has almost doubled since 1990.

G.T.   How will these changes in the climate affect women's human rights in the global South?

U.R.   Experts in the social dimensions of climate change think in terms of 'vulnerability, adaptation and mitigation'. Let's look at vulnerability first. Most experts on the effects of climate change predict that poor people in the global South will be the worst hit by climate change, because they have fewer resources and options. We already know that women form the majority of the world's poor, so we can predict that they will suffer disproportionately. We already know too, from catastrophes like the terrible Bangladesh cyclone of 1991 and the 2004 tsunami, that extreme events often kill women in greater numbers than men; in other words, women are more vulnerable. The TV pictures of displaced people crowded into the New Orleans Superdome after Hurricane Katrina showed mainly African-American women and their children, and we saw elderly white women stranded in their care homes. The fact that most of the people left behind to fend for themselves were women was not remarked on in the media, although the fact that most were African-American was.

G.T. How do you explain women's greater vulnerability to extreme climate events?

U.R. There are many reasons. Most are related to general social and cultural patterns such as the division of labour between men and women, women's responsibility for children, the fact that they tend to have fewer skills and resources than men, and in some cases cultural strictures about women staying secluded in the home – purdah. For instance, as the 1991 cyclone struck in Bangladesh, many women were frightened to break purdah by fleeing their houses for the cyclone shelters. They waited at home for their menfolk to escort them to safety, with the result that the death toll was five times higher for women than for men.

Although the 2004 tsunami was caused by an undersea earthquake and was nothing to do with climate change, it is still instructive for predicting how floods due to global warming might affect women and men differently. It is said that more women died because they were at home with their children while their husbands were away inland on business, they could not swim, and they were trying to protect or rescue their children.

It is not invariably true that women are more vulnerable to climatic catastrophes, though. During Hurricane Mitch, which devastated parts of Central America in 1998, more men than women died. Apparently, that was because the regional culture of machismo led many men into high-risk, 'heroic' behaviour. As well as vulnerability due to the event itself, women may be more vulnerable than men in the social breakdown that often follows a catastrophe. For instance, the tsunami led to a rise in domestic violence in at least one country where it struck, Sri Lanka.

G.T.   Is it just the extreme climate events that will have an impact on women's human rights, or will there be more subtle effects too?

U.R.   As well as sudden extreme events like hurricanes and floods, climate change is predicted to cause droughts in some parts of the global South; indeed, it seems as if this is already happening, for instance in parts of Africa. This will have a knock-on effect on the work burdens of women and girls. First, they are usually responsible for obtaining water for the family, and drought will make this task harder and more time-consuming.

Drought will also lead to lower crop yields in the tropics, and greater risk of famine. Global warming may have caused the 2005 famine in Niger. Women are responsible for 70–80 per cent of food production in sub-Saharan Africa, 65 per cent in Asia and 45 per cent in Latin America and the Caribbean, and they have the main responsibility for feeding children. Declines in food production, and famines, will hit them hard. As well as struggling with the immediate effects of famine and chronic food shortages, women will have to be involved in 'adaptation', choosing different crops or finding new agricultural methods. Yet government agricultural extension services that could teach women these things are usually directed at men.

If clean drinking water becomes scarce, that will lead to an increase in water-borne diseases, and because it is usually women who look after sick family-members, this will again increase their workload. If poor women in the global South have to spend even more time on such work than they do already, that means less time and energy for earning an independent income, learning to read or getting involved in local politics, all of which puts basic human rights further out of their reach.

G.T.   Does global policy making on climate change take these issues into account?

U.R.   As yet, comparatively little research has been done on how poor women will be affected by climate change, although interest is growing. As for international negotiations on ways of cutting emissions and reducing the warming effect, 'mitigation' in other words, very few women are involved. International decision making on mitigation must take the interests of poor women in the global South and the rest of the world into account, and apply the 'polluter pays' principle – after all, poor women did not cause this problem.

What next for poor women's human rights? Some suggestions

So, what next? Surveying the many ways in which poor women's human rights are denied, violated or menaced can give rise to feelings of dismay and helplessness as well as frustration. But, in my view, that would be mistaken, as well as counterproductive. It is precisely because of the work of activists over the last 40 years that we can even recognise the discrimination poor women have to contend with. It has taken the arduous, ground-breaking and sometimes dangerous efforts of thousands of women to make a book like this conceivable.

It is certainly true that poverty and suffering has deepened for many poor women in the South, as a result of economic structural adjustment, the debt crisis, HIV/AIDS, the rise in dowry-related violence in India and other trends. And let us not forget the millions of 'missing women', who were denied even the right to life because of their sex. As victories have been achieved, new challenges have emerged, so that sometimes it seems like running to stay in the same place. On the other hand, poor women's rights are getting onto the development and human rights agendas, although they are still not taken seriously enough by the international community, governments and many elements of civil society.

The key to ending the unnecessary suffering and poverty caused by discrimination against poor women in the South is their becoming empowered to claim their rights. I hope this book will motivate you to want to get involved in supporting this in some way, if you are not already doing so. There are plenty of practical things you can do:

◆ Support an international development charity that takes women's human rights seriously and prioritises work to assist poor women's empowerment, in fields such as poverty reduction, education, HIV/AIDS and so on. Some useful websites are listed under 'Resources'.

◆ If you already support an international development charity, find out what it is doing to support poor women's empowerment. If you are not satisfied with the answer, ask them to do more.

◆ Join a membership organisation concerned with women's human rights, especially one that works internationally and is part of a global network. This should enable you to become involved in campaigning activities as well as keeping you up to date with new developments.

◆ Get involved in one of the campaigns dedicated to addressing women's pay and conditions in the South, such as Oxfam's Make Trade Fair campaign.

◆ If you are already involved in a movement or campaign concerned with global justice, for instance, an environmental campaign, think about how women's human rights are involved, and raise the issue with other activists whenever you can. It is vital to help people realise that women's rights are pivotal to many of today's pressing causes.

◆ As a consumer, you can help by thinking about what you are buying, and finding out what role women have played in producing or making it. Boycotts are rarely the answer to women's labour rights abuses, as they could end up throwing workers into destitution. Instead, buy fair trade products if and when you can, but also try to find out whether or not the fair trade body concerned is working to promote the rights of the women involved. If the answer seems to be 'no', ask why not.

Resources

1: Interconnections

Asociación Aurora Vivar
See WOMANKIND Worldwide website (details below). There
is also information on the Spanish-language website Gloobal
<www.gloobal.info/iepala>.

Association for Women's Rights in Development (AWID)
<www.awid.org>
AWID is an international membership organisation connecting,
informing and mobilising people and organisations committed to
achieving gender equality, sustainable development and women's
human rights. About half of the members are based in the global
South or in Eastern Europe. Its goal is to cause policy, institu-
tional and individual change that will improve the lives of women
and girls everywhere. Since 1982, AWID has been doing this by
facilitating on-going debates on fundamental and provocative
issues, as well as by building the individual and organisational
capacities of those working for women's empowerment.

British Broadcasting Corporation (BBC) <www.bbc.co.uk>
The BBC's news service carries interesting stories touching on
rights and development issues from all over the world, and is
a very good source of information on women's rights issues.

British Council <www.britishcouncil.org>
The Council has worked in development for over 40 years,
specialising in education and training, governance, economic

development and health. It currently manages over 100 contracts funded by more than 20 agencies in Asia, Africa, the Middle East and Eastern and Central Europe.

Development Alternatives with Women for a New Era (DAWN) <www.dawnorg.org>

DAWN is a network of women scholars and activists from the global South who engage in feminist research and analysis of the global environment and are committed to working for economic justice, gender justice and democracy.

Masimanyane Women's Support Centre <www.masimanyane.org.za>

Masimanyane Women's Support Centre is a non-profit international women's organisation based in East London, South Africa. It promotes the domestic implementation of international human rights standards by building the capacity of women and human rights advocates to claim and realise women's human rights.

Oxfam Great Britain <www.oxfam.org.uk>

Oxfam Great Britain's goal is a world where every person is secure, skilled, equal, safe, healthy and heard. It is an independent British organisation, registered as a charity, affiliated to Oxfam International, with partners, volunteers, supporters and staff of many nationalities.

Oxfam International <www.oxfam.org>

Oxfam International is a confederation of 13 organisations working together with over 3000 partners in more than 100 countries to find lasting solutions to poverty, suffering and injustice. With many of the causes of poverty global in nature, the 13 affiliate members of Oxfam International believe they can achieve greater impact through their collective efforts. Oxfam International seeks increased worldwide public understanding that economic and social justice are crucial to sustainable development. It strives to be a global campaigning force promoting the awareness and motivation that come with global citizenship, whilst seeking to shift public opinion in order to give equity the same priority as economic growth.

Panos Institute <www.panos.org.uk>

The principal aims of the London-based Panos Institute are to illuminate and provide insights from developing countries into issues facing us globally, and to stimulate informed, enlightened discussion around such issues. Panos sets out to make the immensely complex issues facing developing countries accessible and understandable, to provide information that people can trust, and to open up opportunities for different perspectives to be understood.

United Nations Development Fund for Women (UNIFEM) <www.unifem.org>

UNIFEM is the women's fund at the United Nations. It provides financial and technical assistance to innovative programmes and strategies to foster women's empowerment and gender equality.

WOMANKIND Worldwide <www.womankind.org.uk>

WOMANKIND Worldwide believes women in developing countries are a powerful force for change, and that they have an abundance of practical ideas for improving their own lives and lifting their families and communities out of poverty. But this can only happen if they have the confidence and opportunities to articulate their needs and ideas and be listened to. WOMANKIND Worldwide is the only UK charity devoted to enabling women to achieve this.

2: **Women's human rights: a closer look**

Amnesty International (AI) <www.amnesty.org>
AI is a worldwide movement of people who campaign for internationally recognised human rights. AI's vision is of a world in which every person enjoys all of the human rights enshrined in the Universal Declaration of Human Rights and other international human rights standards.

Human Rights Watch (HRW) <www.hrw.org>
HRW is an independent, non-governmental organisation, supported by contributions from private individuals and foundations worldwide. HRW is dedicated to protecting the human rights of people around the world.

United Nations High Commissioner for Human Rights <www.unhchr.org>
The United Nations vision is of a world in which the human rights of all are fully respected and enjoyed in conditions of global peace. The High Commissioner works to keep that vision to the forefront through constant encouragement of the international community and its member states to uphold universally agreed human rights standards.

WHRnet <www.Whrnet.org>
WHRnet aims to provide reliable, comprehensive and timely information and analyses on women's human rights in English, Spanish and French. The site provides updates on women's human rights issues and policy developments globally, and provides information and analyses that support advocacy actions.

3: The threat of cultural relativism

Association for Women's Rights in Development
See under Section 1

PATH <www.path.org>
PATH is a US-based international, non-profit organisation that creates sustainable, culturally relevant solutions, enabling communities worldwide to break longstanding cycles of poor health. It collaborates with public and private-sector partners to help provide appropriate health technologies and vital strategies that change the way people think and act.

4: 'Not a fax from heaven'

Baobab for Women's Human Rights
<www.baobabwomen.org>
Baobab For Women's Human Rights is a not-for-profit, non-governmental women's human rights organisation, which focuses on women's legal rights issues under the three systems of law in Nigeria: customary, statutory and religious laws. Baobab operates from a national office in Lagos and with outreach teams in 14 states across Nigeria. It works with women, legal and paralegal professionals, human rights NGOs and members of the general public.

Catholics for a Free Choice (CFFC)
<www.catholicsforchoice.org>
CFFC was founded in 1973 to serve as a voice for Catholics who believe that the Catholic tradition supports a woman's moral and legal right to follow her conscience in matters of sexuality and reproductive health. CFFC is based in Washington D.C. and works with sister organisations in various other countries, including several in Latin America.

Women Against Fundamentalisms (WAF)
<www.waf.gn.apc.org>

WAF was launched in 1989 to challenge the rise of fundamentalism in all religions. WAF believes that fundamentalism appears
in different and changing forms in religions throughout the
world, sometimes as a state project, sometimes in opposition to
the state. At the heart of all fundamentalist agendas is the
control of women's minds and bodies.

Women Living Under Muslim Laws (WLUML)
<www.wluml.org>

WLUML is an international solidarity network that provides
information, support and a collective space for women whose
lives are shaped, conditioned or governed by laws and customs said to derive from Islam. Established over 20 years ago,
WLUML now extends to more than 70 countries ranging
from South Africa to Uzbekistan, Senegal to Indonesia and
Brazil to France. The network aims to strengthen women's
individual and collective struggles for equality and their rights,
especially in Muslim contexts.

5: The podium and the polling booth

Inter-Parliamentary Union (IPU) <www.ipu.org>

The IPU is the international organisation of parliaments of
sovereign states. Based in Geneva, it is the focal point for
worldwide parliamentary dialogue and works for peace and
cooperation among peoples and for the firm establishment of
representative democracy. The IPU supports the efforts of the
United Nations, whose objectives it shares, and works in close
cooperation with it. The website has information on the per-
centages of women in national parliaments, and a 'Women in
politics' database.

Royal Tropical Institute, Netherlands <www.kit.nl>
The Royal Tropical Institute is an independent Dutch not-for-profit organisation, a centre of knowledge and expertise in the areas of international and intercultural cooperation. The aims are to contribute to sustainable development, poverty alleviation, and cultural preservation and exchange, and gender is a key theme.

6: Women's economic rights in a globalising world

Chinese Working Women Network (CWWN) <www.cwwn.org>
The CWWN was set up in 1996 as a non-governmental organisation. Its goal is to help Chinese migrant women workers within China to fight for alternative and sustainable development. The network brings together labour organisers, feminists, university professors, researchers, social workers, cultural activists, workers and students.

Clean Clothes Campaign (CCC) <www.cleanclothes.org>
The CCC is an international campaign focused on improving working conditions in the global garment and sportswear industries. There are Clean Clothes Campaigns in Austria, Belgium, France, Germany, the Netherlands, Spain, Sweden, Switzerland and the United Kingdom.

Gender Responsive Budget Initiatives <www.gender-budgets.org>
The GRBI website is a collaborative effort between the United Nations Development Fund for Women (UNIFEM), The Commonwealth Secretariat and Canada's International Development Research Centre (IDRC), to support government and civil society in analysing national and/or local budgets from a gender perspective and applying this analysis to the formulation

of gender responsive budgets. The initiative strives to promote the global objectives and cross-regional information sharing through the formation/support of a network, further development of concepts, tools and training materials, global training of trainers, South–South exchanges, and collaboration with international and regional organizations.

International Gender and Trade Network (IGTN) <www.igtn.org>

IGTN is a Southern-led network of feminist gender specialists who provide technical information on gender and trade issues to women's groups, NGOs, social movements and governments. IGTN acts as a political catalyst to enlarge the space for a critical feminist perspective and global action on trade and globalisation issues.

Kuapa Kokoo <www.kuapakokoogh.com>

Kuapa Kokoo is a cocoa farmers' co-operative organisation that works to improve the lot of its members. It was established in 1993. Kuapa Kokoo is a composite organisation with five main sub-groups, including the Day Chocolate Company, based in London.

Oxfam Australia <www.oxfam.org.au>

Oxfam Australia is an independent, not-for-profit, secular, community-based aid and development organisation working in 31 countries. It has been a member of the Oxfam International family since 1995. It works in partnership with local communities to end poverty and injustice, in keeping with its vision of a fair world in which people control their own lives, their basic rights are achieved and the environment is sustained.

Social Watch <socialwatch.org>

Social Watch is an international NGO watchdog network monitoring poverty eradication and gender equality.

Women in Development Europe (WIDE)
<www.eurosur.org/wide>
WIDE is a European network of development NGOs, gender specialists and human rights activists. It monitors and influences international economic and development policy and practice from a feminist perspective. Its work is grounded on women's rights as the basis for the development of a more just and democratic world order.

Women's Edge Coalition <www.womensedge.org>
The US-based Women's Edge Coalition advocates international economic policies and human rights that support women worldwide in their actions to end poverty in their lives, communities and nations.

Women Working Worldwide
<www.poptel.org.uk/women-ww>
Women Working Worldwide is a UK-based organisation which works with an international network of women workers' organisations, and women's projects within trade unions. The focus is on supporting the rights of women working in international production chains that supply the UK and other European countries with consumer goods such as food and clothing.

Worker Rights Consortium (WRC)
<www.workersrights.org>
The WRC is a non-profit organisation created by college and university administrations, students and labour rights experts in the United States. The WRC's purpose is to assist in the enforcement of manufacturing codes of conduct adopted by colleges and universities.

7: 'Sowing a seed': the right to education

ActionAid International <www.actionaid.org>

An international development agency, ActionAid works with local partners to fight poverty and injustice worldwide, helping them fight for and gain their rights to food, shelter, work, education, health care and a voice in the decisions that affect their lives.

Beyond Access Project
<http://ioewebserver.ioe.ac.uk/ioe/cms/get.asp?cid=7746>

The Beyond Access Project is a joint initiative of the Institute of Education and Oxfam GB. The project aims to contribute to achieving the Millennium Development Goal of promoting gender equality by critically examining knowledge about how to achieve gender equitable basic education.

Campaign for Female Education (CAMFED) International
<www.camfed.org>

CAMFED supports girls in rural areas of Zimbabwe, Zambia, Ghana and Tanzania, helping them to complete primary and secondary education and encouraging school leavers to become the next generation of social and business entrepreneurs. It supports girls in Africa because they are the poorest people in the world with the least opportunities. CAMFED's vision is of a world in which every child is educated, protected, respected and valued, and grows up to turn the tide of poverty.

Global Campaign for Education (GCE)
<www.campaignforeducation.org>

Founded in 1999, the GCE brings together NGOs and teachers' unions from all over the world to promote education as a basic human right. The campaign mobilises public pressure on governments and the international community to fulfil their promises to provide free, compulsory, public, basic education for everyone, in particular for children, women and all disadvantaged, deprived sections of society.

United Nations Emergency Fund for Children (UNICEF)
<www.unicef.org>
UNICEF's priority areas are girls' education, immunisation and child health, child protection, HIV/AIDS and children and early childhood. There is a large section on girls' education under 'What we do'.

8: The violence against women pandemic

Demus <www.demus.org.pe>
A Peruvian NGO, Demus lobbies government and civil society to ensure they fulfil their responsibilities in relation to women's human rights.

Masimanyane Women's Support Centre
See resources for Section 1

Project Against Domestic Violence (PADV)
<http://padvcambodia.org/>
PADV is a Cambodian NGO that works to prevent, reduce and eliminate domestic violence, and to help its victims.

We Can End Violence Against Women
<www.wecanendvaw.org>
The We Can alliance is a growing coalition of over 400 organisations, collectives and individuals in Bangladesh, Sri Lanka, India, Nepal, Pakistan and Afghanistan who have joined efforts to end violence against women. The campaign seeks to achieve a fundamental shift in attitudes and beliefs that support violence against women, a collective and visible stand against violence against women, and popular support to end violence against women.

White Ribbon Campaign (WRC) <www.whiteribbon.ca>
The WRC, based in Canada, describes itself as the largest effort in the world of men working to end men's violence against women. It relies on volunteer support and financial contributions from individuals and organisations.

World Health Organization (WHO) <www.who.org>
The World Health Organization (WHO) is the United Nations specialised agency for health. WHO's objective, as set out in its constitution, is the attainment by all peoples of the highest possible level of health. It defines health as a state of complete physical, mental and social well-being, and not merely the absence of disease or infirmity.

9: Women's rights abuses help to spread HIV/AIDS

International HIV/AIDS Alliance <www.aidsalliance.org>
The International HIV/AIDS Alliance is an initiative of people, organisations and communities working towards a shared vision by supporting effective community responses to HIV and AIDS. The Alliance believes that those at the forefront of the HIV/AIDS response need to have the resources to take on the challenges that the epidemic presents. It is the European Union's largest HIV/AIDS-focused development organisation, and has become established as a leading player in the global response to the epidemic.

The Joint United Nations Programme on HIV/AIDS (UNAIDS) <www.unaids.org>
UNAIDS's mission is to lead, strengthen and support an expanded response to HIV and AIDS that includes preventing transmission of HIV, providing care and support to those already living with the virus, reducing the vulnerability of individuals and communities to HIV and alleviating the impact of the epidemic.

10: The future is already happening

Association for Women's Rights in Development
See resources for Section 1

Focal point gender, environment, sustainability (Genanet)
<www.genanet.de>
Genanet aims to integrate gender justice in environmental and
sustainability policy. It provides information on the gender
aspects of environmental issues, carries out studies, advises
environmental organisations and institutions on how to integrate gender aspects into their work, and is active in various
working groups and networks. Although it mainly focuses on
Germany, it also works at European and international levels.
By developing sustainable and gender-just lifestyles in the
North and addressing global equity issues, Genanet hopes to
support sustainable livelihood in the South too.

Notes

Chapter 1: Interconnections

1. These figures are from a range of sources, including WOMANKIND World-wide www.womankind.org.uk and the Inter-Parliamentary Union www.ipu.org.

2. Information in this story is taken from: We Can end violence campaign website <www.wecanendvaw.org>; 'Bengal Tribesmen Kill "Witches",' *BBC News*, 1 August 2002 <http://news.bbc.co.uk/1/hi/world/south_asia/2166856.stm>; and 'Indian Mob Burns "Witches",' *BBC News*, 3 July 2003 <http://news.bbc.co.uk/1/hi/world/south_asia/3040804.stm>.

3. *Our Common Interest: Report of Commission for Africa*, March 2005 <http://www.issafrica.org/Af/RegOrg/unity_to_union/cfarep.htm> (executive summary available on <http://www.worldfooddayusa.org/?id=16363>).

4. *Analysis of the Commission for Africa Report*, UK Gender and Develop-ment Network, April 2005.

5. Peggy Antrobus is a founder member of Development Alternatives for Women in the New Era (DAWN). Her comment is cited in Diane Elson, *The Millennium Development Goals: A Feminist Development Economics Perspective*, address delivered on 7 October 2004 on the occasion of the 52nd anniversary of the Institute of Social Studies, The Hague, the Netherlands.

6. *Equals* Newsletter for Beyond Access: Gender, Education and Development, Issue No. 14, September-October 2005. See <www.ioewebserver .ioe.ac.uk> and follow the links.

7. On a more positive note, more targets have been added.

8. *The Cost of Childbirth: How Women are Paying the Price for Broken Promises on Aid*, Oxfam Briefing Paper 52, March 2004.

9. Commission on Macro-Economics and Health, cited in *The Cost of Childbirth*, p. 2.

10. *The Millennium Development Goals Report 2005*, United Nations, New York, 2005, p. 22.

11. The World Bank's study *Voices of the Poor* documents dialogues with 60,000 poor people in 50 countries, and contains valuable information

about how poor men and women perceive and experience poverty. But, while the interviews themselves show that men and women tend to experience poverty in different ways, this crucial point is not made in the overall report. See Gerd Johnsson-Latham, *"Ecce Homo?" Gender Based Discrimination as a Reason for Poverty*, Swedish Ministry for Foreign Affairs, June 2002.

12. Mahbub ul Haq *What is Human Development?* from the Human Development Reports page of the United Nations Development Programme website <http://hdr.undp.org/hd>.

13. http://www.oxfam.org.uk/what_we_do/where_we_work/pakistan/hand pumps/handpump.htm.

14. *No Country Treats its Women the Same as its Men: The Gender Equity Index – A New Perspective*, Social Watch, 19 August 2005 <http://www.socialwatch.org/en/informeImpreso/pdfs/gei2005_eng.pdf>.

15. 'Dowry violence' is the use of violence against a wife by the husband and his family in order to extract larger dowries from the wife's family after the marriage.

16. Rahul Bedi 'Jail Crisis for Dowry Crimes,' *BBC News*, 1 June 2000 <http://news.bbc.co.uk/1/hi/world/south_asia/772896.stm>.

17. See, for example, Lucy Ash 'India's dowry deaths,' *BBC News*, 16 July 2003 <http://news.bbc.co.uk/1/hi/programmes/crossing_continents/3071963.stm>.

18. 'Thanking TV for little girls,' *The Age*, 27 September 2003 <http://www.theage.com.au/articles/2003/09/26/1064083186832.html?f rom=storyrhs>.

19. 'You have come a long way, baby,' *Times of India News Network*, 14 March 2005 <www.search.indiatimes.com>.

20. Mabel Mulimo et al., *Zambia Strategic Country Gender Assessment*, World Bank, June 2004, p. 12.

21. Jay Goulden and Sarah Glyde, *Development of a Rights-Based Monitoring Tool for CARE Malawi*, CARE, March 2004.

22. Naila Kabeer *Reversed Realities: Gender Hierarchies in Development Thought*, Verso, London, 1994; cited in Jo Rowlands, *Questioning Empowerment: Working with Women in Honduras*, Oxfam, Oxford, 1997, p. 22.

23. Organisations working on trafficking issues estimate that thousands of women and children are trafficked each year out of Nepal into neighbouring countries, primarily to India. It is estimated that close to 200,000 women and girls from Nepal are working under oppressive conditions in the red light areas of Indian cities such as Bombay.

24. From a presentation given at the *Gender Myths* conference at the Institute of Development Studies, Sussex, UK, in July 2003.

25. 'The Policy Framework for Implementing MDG3,' statement by Ms Rachel Mayanja, Assistant Secretary-General and Special Adviser to the Secretary-General on Gender Issues and Advancement of Women, at the High-level

Consultation *Promoting the Gender Equality MDG: The Implementation Challenge* at the World Bank, Washington D.C., 16 February 2006.

26. Heather Grady is now Director of 'Policy and Partnerships, Realizing Rights' at the Ethical Globalization Initiative.

27. AVV is part of a South American network that organised the public tribunal on women´s economic and social rights in different countries, supported by Oxfam.

28. Personal communication.

29. Personal communication.

2: Women's human rights: a closer look

1. 'Message of the High Commissioner', 4 December 1998 <www.unhchr. ch/huricane/huricane.nsf/view01/9854502F4BBA4EF9802566D00053E A61?opendocument

2. In this case, discrimination takes the form of parents' preference for boys, lack of opportunities for girls apart from marriage, and the custom of marrying girls off early.

3. Amartya Sen, 'Human Rights and Asian Values: What Lee Kuan Yew and Li Peng don't understand about Asia,' *The New Republic*, 14 July 1997, Vol. 217 Nos 2–3.

4. Article 2, Universal Declaration of Human Rights <www.un.org/Overview/rights.html>.

5. In the case of treaties, I have given the dates they entered into force, rather than the dates they were adopted and opened for signature. Conventions need a certain number of signatures from states before they enter into force.

6. Article 18, Vienna Declaration and Programme of Action <www.ohchr.org/english/law/vienna.htm>.

7. Article 1 of CEDAW <www.un.org/womenwatch/daw/cedaw>.

8. Speech at Womankind Worldwide/British Council conference *Global Challenges to Women's Human Rights: 25 years of CEDAW*, 9 December 2004, London.

9. 'The Convention on the Elimination of All Forms of Discrimination against Women' and the Optional Protocol *Women's Rights and Economic Change*, No. 2, August 2002, Association for Women's Rights in Development See <http://www.awid.org/publications/primers/factsis sues2.pdf> and <http://www.un.org/womenwatch/daw/cedaw>.

10. WOMANKIND Worldwide/British Council conference *Global Challenges to Women's Human Rights: 25 years of CEDAW*, 9 December 2004, London.

11. The Optional Protocol came into force in 2000. At the time of writing, 78 countries have adopted it.

12. 'At Beijing+10 Women Beat Back A Bush Offensive and Get the Platform

for Action Reaffirmed,' in *News and Views*, Women's Environment and Development Organization, Vol. 1, No. 1, June 2005.

13. The term 'dowry murders' refers to the murder of women in India and Bangladesh because their parents have not fulfilled their dowry promises or have not responded to demands for more money from the husband and his family.

14. This point is taken from U.A. O'Hare 'Realizing Human Rights for Women,' in *Human Rights Quarterly*, Johns Hopkins University Press, Vol. 21, 1999, pp. 364–402.

15. From 'What's New at WHRNet,' WHRnet Bulletin, 24 October 2004 <www.whrnet.org>.

16. Maxine Molyneux and Shahra Razavi (eds), *Gender Justice, Development and Rights*, Oxford University Press, Oxford, 2002).

17. Speech at Womankind Worldwide/British Council conference *Global Challenges to Women's Human Rights: 25 years of CEDAW*, 9 December 2004, London.

18. From Dzodzi Tsikata, 'Gender Mainstreaming to a Rights Based Approach: What is New and What does it Mean for Gender Equality Policy Making?' in *Repositioning Feminisms in Development*, Institute of Development Studies Bulletin, Vol. 35 No. 4, October 2004.

19. Centre for Women's Global Leadership, 'Vienna + 10: Speak Out – Help Shape the Future of Women's Human Rights' <www.cwgl.rutgers.edu/globalcenter/vienna10>.

20. Devaka Jain, 'Women's Rights between the UN Human Rights Framework and Free Trade Agreements,' in Mandy Macdonald (ed.), *Globalising Women's Rights; Confronting Unequal Development Between the UN Rights Framework and the WTO Trade Agreements, Report of Women in Development Europe's Annual Conference 2004*, p. 11.

21. The information about Activa draws on an article by Ana Maria Arteaga, 'Yes to Equality – Right Now!' in *Links*, Oxfam, May 2005.

22. Speech at *Womankind Worldwide/British Council conference Global Challenges to Women's Human Rights: 25 years of CEDAW*, 9 December 2004, London.

Chapter 3. The threat of cultural relativism

1. Cited in Abdullah A. An-Nai'im (ed.), *Cultural Transformation and Human Rights in Africa*, Zed Books, London and New York, 2002.

2. Fatima L. Adamu, 'A Double-edged Sword: Challenging Women's Oppression within Muslim Society in Northern Nigeria,' in *Gender and Development*, Vol. 7, No. 1, March 1999.

3. This observation is based on my experience during a stay of several weeks in Mundgod in 2000.

4. Maree Stacey 'Religion, Male Violence and the Control of Women: Pakistani Muslim Men in Bradford, UK,' in *Gender and Development*, Vol. 7, No. 1, Oxfam, March 1999, p. 52.

5. Statement made by Deniz Kandiyoti of the School of Oriental and African Studies during discussion at the *Gender Myths* conference, Institute of Development Studies, Sussex, UK, July 2003.

6. Based on an article by Eno-Obong Akpan, 'Early Marriage in Eastern Nigeria and the Health Consequences of Vesico-vaginal Fistulae (VVF) among Young Mothers,' in *Gender and Development*, Vol. 11, No. 2, Oxfam, July 2003.

7. Ibid. According to *WHO Newsletter* 17(2), cited by Akpan, only 6.5 per cent of the population have access to health care <http://www.dnetsystem sllc.net/whongr/quarter/maternal.html>.

8. Roland Buerk, 'The Crisis of Bangladesh's Garment Trade,' *BBC News*, 14 June 2004 <http://news.bbc.co.uk/1/hi/world/south_asia/3798149.stm>.

9. Maitrayee Mukhopadhyay, 'Gender Relations, Development and Culture,' *Gender and Development*, Vol. 3, No. 1, 1995, Oxfam, cited in Susie Jolly, *Gender and Cultural Change: Overview report*, BRIDGE Development–Gender, Institute of Development Studies, July 2002.

10. Beijing Platform for Action, paragraph 97 <www.un.org/womenwatch/daw/beijing/platform>.

11. Association for Women's Rights in Development, Eradicating Female Genital Mutilation, Kathambi Kinoti, 15 April 2005. <http://www.awid.org/go.php?stid=1466>.

12. This case study was compiled from several sources. The main one was Kathambi Kinoti, *Eradicating Female Genital Mutilation: Sexuality Rights vs Cultural relativism*, Association for Women's Rights in Development, 15 April 2005 <www.awid.org/go.php?stid=1466>. Information was also drawn from: 'Kenya: A Case Study of Modern Legislation against Cultural Identity,' IRIN News, UN Office for the Coordination of Humanitarian Affairs, 22 March 2005 <www.irinnews.org/print.asp?ReportID=45979> and 'Circumcision through Words' (a selection of press releases and articles) in *Traditional Music and Cultures of Kenya* <www.bluegecko.org/kenya/tribes/meru/articles-circword.htm>. See also the PATH website <www.path.org>.

Chapter 4: 'Not a fax from heaven'

1. From Women against Fundamentalisms (WAF)'s website <www.waf.gn.apc.org>.

2. I use the term 'fundamentalism' or 'fundamentalist' throughout this chapter because it is in common usage. However, it is important to acknowledge that many religious believers reject the idea that the groups described here represent the core tenets of their faiths.

3. This definition is based on the one given on the Women against Fundamentalisms website <www.waf.gn.apc.org>.

4. Information taken from Alan Johnston, 'Hamas under Pressure over Vigilantes,' BBC News, 19 April 2005 <http://news.bbc.co.uk/1/hi/world/middle_east/4457699.stm> and Independent, 13 April 2005.

5. Religious Fundamentalisms and Sexual and Reproductive Rights (Education Pack), WAF <www.waf.gn.apc.org>.

6. 'Family Planning Row in Guatemala,' BBC News, 2 February 2006 <http://news.bbc.co.uk/1/hi/world/americas/4673160.stm>.

7. 'Pope Rejects Condoms for Africa,' BBC News, 10 June 2005 <http://news.bbc.co.uk/1/hi/world/europe/4081276.stm>.

8. Steve Bradshaw, 'Vatican: Condoms Don't Stop AIDS,' Guardian, 9 October 2003 <www.guardian.co.uk/aids/story/0,7369,1059068,00.html>.

9. 'Cardinal Backs Limited Condom Use,' BBC News, 21 April 2006 <http://news.bbc.co.uk/1/hi/world/europe/4929962.stm>.

10. Frances Kissling, 'The Catholics who Support Choice,' Washington Post, 21 August 1985.

11. William Fisher, 'Condoms Lose Ground in HIV Prevention,' Inter Press Service News Agency, 31 August 2005.

12. Hanaa Edwar, 'Following the Sit-in,' in 'Iraqi Women Concerned about Rights,' Currents, July/August 2005, UNIFEM <www.unifem.org>.

13. Fatou Sow, 'Many Worlds in Different Places,' presentation at the inaugural DAWN Training Institute, Bangalore, in DAWN Special Supplement for the World Social Forum, Mumbai, 16–21 January 2004. <www.guardian.co.uk/pakistan/Story/0,2763,1548190,00.html>.

14. Based on extracts from 'Gender expert Musdah speaks within reason,' Jakarta Post, 7 October 2004. See <www.wluml.org/english/newsfulltxt.shtml?cmd%5B157%5D=x-157-75549>.

Chapter 5: The podium and the polling booth

1. Figures from Inter-Parliamentary Union (IPU), showing the picture on 30 November 2006. See its website <www.ipu.org> for this and more data on women in parliaments.

2. From Creating Laws to Combat Violence against Women, United Nations Development Fund for Women (UNIFEM), 1 December 2003 <www.unifem.org>.

3. Progress of the World's Women 2002, UNIFEM <www.unifem.org>.

4. See 'Loans, Literacy and Lobbying,' Oxfam website <www.oxfam.org.uk/what_we_do/issues/democracy_rights/story_mali.htm>.

5. Declan Walsh, 'The place where women risk their lives to run for office,' Guardian, 13 August 2005 <www.guardian.co.uk>.

6. *Take the Guns Away: Afghan Voices on Security and Elections*, The Human Rights Research and Advocacy Consortium, September 2004.

7. Tom Coghlan, 'Election Hopes of Afghan Women,' *BBC News*, 14 August 2005
    <http://news.bbc.co.uk/1/hi/world/south_asia/4144760.stm>.

8. *Campaigning against Fear: Women's Participation in Afghanistan's 2005 Elections*, Human Rights Watch, 2005, p. 12 <http://hrw.org/back grounder/wrd/afghanistan0805/index.htm>.

9. 'Afghan Women's Poll Money Issue,' *BBC News*, 26 August 2005
    <http://news.bbc.co.uk/1/hi/world/south_asia/4189034.stm>.

10. Tom Coghlan, 'Election Hopes of Afghan Women,' *BBC News*, 14 August 2005.

11. Tom Coghlan, 'Election Hopes of Afghan Women.'

12. 'Heard,' Case Study Guatemala, Oxfam
    <www.oxfam.co.uk/about_us/thisisoxfam/heard/case_study.htm>.

13. For a very good overview of women's quota systems, see Mary-Ann Stephenson, *Gender and Democracy: What Works? Strategies to Increase Women's Representation*, British Council, UK, 2004.

14. The information here is taken from several sources: Okao Joel Tema, 'Rwanda: Women of the house,' *Panos London Online,* 12 April 2005; Grace Mukagabiro, 'Rwanda never again: UN must act now,' Oxfam <www.oxfam.org.uk/what_we_do/issues/conflict_disasters/art_unsum mit.htm>; 'Rwanda Moves to Top Women MP list,' *BBC News,* 22 October 2003 <http://news.bbc.co.uk/1/hi/world/africa/3204401.stm>; and Elizabeth Powley, *Strengthening Governance: The Role of Women in Rwanda's Transition*, Women Waging Peace and The Policy Commission, October 2003.

15. The quotations and other information relating to COVA are taken from Maitrayee Mukhopadhyay and Shamim Meer, 'Building Political Legitimacy for Elected Muslim, Dalit and Backward Caste Women: Confederation of Voluntary Associations (COVA)' in *Creating Voice and Crossing Space: Redefining Governance from a Gender Perspective,* Royal Tropical Institute, the Netherlands, 2004, pp. 88–93.

Chapter 6: Women's economic rights in a globalising world

1. 'Women's Rights, the World Trade Organization and International Trade Policy,' *Women's Rights and Economic Change,* No. 4, Association for Women's Rights in Development, August 2002 <www.awid.org/publica tions/primers/factsissues4.pdf>.

2. 'Goal 1: Eradicate extreme poverty and hunger,' in *Millennium Development Goals Report 2005*, World Bank 2005, pp. 6–7.

3. This figure is taken from the United States Agency for International Development (USAID) website <www.usaid.gov>.

4. There are four key ILO conventions relating to gender equality at work: the Equal Remuneration Convention (1951), the Discrimination (Employment and Occupation) Convention (1958), the Workers with Family Responsibilities Convention (1981) and the Maternity Protection Convention (2000).

5. 'Overview: Women, Work and Poverty,' p. 3, in *Progress of the Word's Women 2005*, UNIFEM, 2005.

6. 'Gender Equality Fact Sheet,' from State of the World's Population 2005, United Nations Family Planning Association, p. 9
   <http://www.unfpa.org/swp/2005/presskit/factsheets/facts_gender.htm>.

7. See *Making A Living* October 2003 on <www.oxfam.org.uk/what_we_do/where_we_work/angola/makingaliving.htm>.

8. Pamela Caro, *Consequences and Costs of Precarious Employment for Women Workers in the Agro-exports Sector*, a report prepared within Oxfam's Global Trade Campaign on Labour Rights, June 2003, p. 3.

9. *Trading Away Our Rights: Women Working in Global Supply Chains*, Oxfam, 2004, p. 78.

10. Maria Hartl, *Rural Women's Access to Land and Property in Selected Countries: Progress Towards Achieving the Aims of the Convention on the Elimination of all Forms of Discrimination against Women*, Food and Agriculture Organization, International Fund for Agricultural Development and the International Land Coalition, June 2004.

11. *A Round For Free: How Rich Countries are Getting a Free Ride on Agricultural Subsidies at the WTO*, Oxfam Briefing Paper 76, Oxfam International, June 2005.

12. Zo Randriamaro, *Gender and Trade: Overview Report*, BRIDGE Development–Gender, Institute of Development Studies, UK, 2006, p. 22.

13. *What happened in Hong Kong? Initial analysis of the WTO Ministerial*, Oxfam Briefing Paper 85, December 2005
    <http://www.oxfam.org/en/files/bp85_hongkong/download>.

14. See *June's story* on Oxfam's website <www.oxfam.org.uk/what_we_do/where_we_work/ghana/june_sarpong.htm>.

15. *Dumping without Borders: How US Agricultural Policies are Destroying the Livelihoods of Mexican Corn Farmers*, Oxfam Briefing Paper 50, Oxfam International, 2003.

16. Marceline White, 'Look FIRST from a Gender Perspective: NAFTA and the FTAA,' in *Gender and Development*, Vol. 12 No. 2, Oxfam, p. 44.

17. *International Cooperation at a Crossroads: Aid, Trade and Security in an Unequal World*, Human Development Report 2005, UNDP, 2005, p. 114.

18. *Trading Away Our Rights*, p. 5.

19. Pun Ngai 'Women Workers in Shenzhen Special Economic Zone, China,' in *Gender and Development*, Vol. 12, No. 2, Oxfam, July 2004, p. 32.

20. Attributed to Dirke Busse, Chairman of the North Rhine Textile

Company, in Christa Wichterich, *The Globalized Woman: Reports from a Future of inequality*, Zed Books, London and New York, 2000, p. 3.

21. From an untitled article by Phil Bloomer of Oxfam's Make Trade Fair campaign;
    <www.oxfam.org.uk/what_we_do/issues/trade/art_bloomer_labour.htm>.

22. Jenny Wai-ling Chan, 'The End of the MFA and the Rising Tide of Labour Disputes in China,' *Corporate Social Responsibility in Asia Weekly* Vol. 1, Week 11, 2005, pp. 7 and 11. Can be downloaded from Chinese Working Women Network website <www.cwwn.org/eng/main.html>; follow the 'Archive' link from the home page.

23. *A gender perspective on the 6th World Trade Organisation Ministerial Conference at Hong Kong*, Women in Development Europe, 2006, p. 4 <www.eurosur.org/wide/Globalisation/Post_HK.pdf>.

24. See the Resources section on the Women's Edge Coalition website <www.womensedge.org>.

25. See, for instance, Deborah Clifton 'Promoting equality in Kitgum District,' in *Links*, Oxfam's gender newsletter, July 2005 <http://www.oxfam.org/en/programs/development/ceafrica/uganda_equality>.

26. More information on these stories can be found on Oxfam's website <www.oxfam.org.uk> and in *Links*, Oxfam's newsletter on gender, July 2005, which can also be accessed from the Oxfam website.

27. Sources for Connor include Oxfam Australia evaluation reports and personal communications.

28 <www.oxfam.org.au/campaigns/labour/reports/dialogue.html>

Chapter 7: 'Sowing a seed': the right to education

1. Taken from material provided by CAMFED International <www.camfed.org/camfedannualreport2002.pdf>. See also the story at the end of this chapter.

2. The proportions are 55 per cent in the Middle East and North Africa, 56 per cent in South Asia and 54 per cent in West and Central Africa. The figures quoted in this paragraph are all from *Children Out of School: Measuring Exclusion from Primary Education*, UNESCO Institute for Statistics, 2005.

3. UNESCO Institute for Statistics <www.stats.uis.unesco.org>. Updated 24 February 2006.

4. For a list of the MDGs, see Chapter 1 or <www.developmentgoals.org>.

5. For instance, see Stephan Klasen, *Does Gender Inequality Reduce Growth and Development: Evidence from Cross-country Regressions*, World Bank Working Paper 20779, 1999, <http://siteresources.world bank.org/INTGENDER/Resources/wp7.pdf>.

6. C. Grown, G. Gupta, and A. Kes, *Taking Action: Achieving Gender*

Equality and Empowering Women, Gender Equality Task Force, UN Millennium Project, 2005.

7. *Sixty Million Girls*, Save the Children, September 2005 <www.savethechildren.org.uk/scuk_cache/scuk/cache/cmsattach/3529_schoolbook.pdf>.

8. This point is taken from *Taking Action: Achieving Gender Equality and empowering women*, Task Force on Gender Equality, Millennium Project, UNDP, 2005, p. 5.

9. *Gender Parity in Secondary Education: Are We There Yet?* Fact Sheet No. 5, UNESCO Institute for Statistics, April 2005 <http://www.uis.unesco.org/ev.php?ID=6094_201&ID2=DO_TOPIC>.

10. *The Community School: An Alternative to Early Marriage*, Oxfam <www.oxfam.org.uk>.

11. Raja Bentaouet Kattan and Nicholas Burnett, *User Fees in Primary Education*, The World Bank, July 2004. Available from Global Campaign for Education website <www.campaignforeducation.org>.

12. *Sixty Million Girls*.

13. 'Status of Education for Rural People in Uganda,' presentation by Hon. Geraldine Namirembe Bitamazire (MP), Minister of Education and Sports, Uganda, at *Ministerial Seminar on Education for Rural People in Africa: Policy Lessons, Options and Priorities*, Addis Ababa, Ethiopia, 7–9 September 2005.

14. Patricia Ames, 'When Access is Not Enough: Educational Exclusion of Rural Girls in Peru,' in Sheila Aikman and Elaine Unterhalter (eds.), *Beyond Access: Transforming Policy and Practice for Gender Equality in Education*, Oxfam, 2005.

15. Article 29, Convention on the Rights of the Child <www.unhchr.ch/html/menu3/b/k2crc.htm>.

16. Ainee Shehzad, 'A Cause Worth Fighting For,' in *Equals*, Newsletter for Beyond Access: Gender, Education and Development, No. 12, May–June 2005.

17. *Policy Paralysis: A Call for Action on HIV/AIDS-related Human Rights Abuses against Women and Girls in Africa*, Human Rights Watch, December 2003, p. 21 <http://www.hrw.org/reports/2003/africa1203/>.

18. Sheila Aikman and Ruth Bechtel, 'Combating the Abuse of Girls in School,' in *Links*, Oxfam, May 2005 <http://www.oxfam.org.uk/what_we_do/issues/gender/links/0505upe.htm>.

19. *A Fair Chance: Attaining Gender Equality in Basic Education by 2005*, GCE, September 2003 <www.oxfam.org/en/policy/briefingnotes/doc 030416_education_fairchance>.

20. 'A Change in Attitudes about Education in Pakistan,' (Interview with Ms Zobaida Jalal Federal Minister for Education Pakistan) in *Education Today Newsletter*, UNESCO, January–March 2004

<http://portal.unesco.org/education/en/ev.php-URL_ID=27736&URL_DO=DO_TOPIC&URL_SECTION=201.html>.

21. *Writing the Wrongs: International Benchmarks on Adult Literacy*, GCE, 2005.
22. See Nirantar's website <www.nirantar.net>.
23. Testimonies from members of Reflect groups; see the Reflect-action website <www.reflect-action.org>.
24. CAMFED *Annual Report* 2003–2004, p. 11.

Chapter 8: The violence against women pandemic

1. *Violence Against Women: A Priority Health Issue* (Section on rape and sexual assault) WHO, 1997, p. 1 <www.who.int/gender/violence/vawpriority/en/>.
2. Violence against women by a husband or partner is variously known as domestic violence, intimate partner violence or family violence.
3. *Violence against women*, Fact sheet No. 239, WHO, June 2000 <www.who.int/mipfiles/2269/239-ViolenceAgainstWomen forMIP.pdf>.
4. Household survey on domestic violence, Project Against Domestic Violence (PADV), Cambodia, 1996.
5. 'Candies in Hell,' cited in Gareth Richards '"We're Not from Mars," Nicaraguan Men Against Violence Assert,' *Panos Features*, 1 November 2001 <www.panos.org.uk>.
6. Gary Barker et al., 'How Do We Know if Men have Changed? Promoting and Measuring Attitude Change with Young Men: Lessons from Program H in Latin America,' in S. Ruxton (ed.), *Gender Equality and Men: Learning from Practice*, Oxfam, Oxford, 2004.
7. M. Koenig et al. 'Domestic Violence in Rural Uganda: Evidence from a Community-based Study,' in *Bulletin of the World Health Organisation*, Vol. 81, No. 1, 2003.
8. Amnesty International press release, 5 March 2004.
9. Beijing Platform for Action <www.un.org/womenwatch/daw/beijing/platform/violence.htm>.
10. 'Domestic Violence against Women and Girls,' *Innocenti Digest*, No. 6, June 2000, UNICEF, p. 2.
11. 'ICPD at 10,' *Entre Nous: The European Magazine for Sexual and Reproductive Health*, No. 57, 2003, WHO.
12. *Violence Against Women: A Priority Health Issue – Definition and Scope of the Problem*, WHO, p. 1 <www.who.int/gender/violence/vawpriority/en/>.
13. E.A. Stanko et al., *Counting the Costs: Estimating the Impact of Domestic Violence in the London Borough of Hackney*, Crime Concern, 1998.
14. Amartya Sen, *Development as Freedom*, Oxford University Press, Oxford, 1999.

15. N. Pandey, *Case Study on Female Garment Workers in Bangalore*, Oxfam, Hyderabad, 2003.
16. *Oxfam Impact Report, 2001.*
17. See Gary Barker et al. 'How do We Know if Men have Changed?'
18. See <www.whiteribbon.ca>.
19. Information taken from Michael Kaufman, 'Transforming our Interventions for Gender Equality by Addressing and Involving Men and Boys: A Framework for Analysis and Action,' in Sandy Ruxton (ed.), *Gender Equality and Men*, Oxfam, Oxford, 2004.
20. 'Uganda: Rape Rampant in Largest Northern IDP Camp,' *Reuters Foundation*, 17 June 2005 <www.alertnet.org/thenews/newsdesk>. The camp in question, in Gulu district to the north of Kampala, holds 64,000 people fleeing the 19-year war between the government and the rebel Lord's Resistance Army.
21. 'Testimony: Congolese Rape Victim,' *BBC News*, 26 October 2004 <http://news.bbc.co.uk/1/hi/world/africa/3953883.stm>.
22. 'Report Shows DR Congo Rape Horror,' *BBC News*, 26 October 2004 <http://news.bbc.co.uk/1/hi/world/africa/3953747.stm>.
23. Jackie Martens, 'Congo Rape Victims Seek Solace,' *BBC News*, 24 January 2004 <http://news.bbc.co.uk/1/hi/world/africa/3426273.stm>.
24. CEDAW Committee General Recommendation 19.
25. This example was supplied by Jyoti Sangh, Ahmedabad, to Shipra Jha, Oxfam staff member. In the course of researching this chapter I was sent many such stories.
26. Philomena Peres, chairperson of Karnataka State Women's Commission, quoted in Charles Haviland, 'Indians Rally Against Dowries,' *BBC News*, 28 November 2003
   <http://news.bbc.co.uk/1/hi/world/south_asia/3246786.stm>.
27. These stories and others like them can be found on the We Can end violence campaign website <www.wecanendvaw.org>.
28. Interview by Jenny Enarsson for We Can end violence campaign.

Chapter 9: Women's rights abuses help to spread HIV/AIDS

1. *Violence, Vengeance and Gender*, Centre for the Study of Violence and Reconciliation, Johannesburg, 2001.
2. From an Address by His Excellency Mr Festus Mogae, President of the Republic of Botswana, at the 26th Special Session of the United Nations General Assembly on HIV/AIDS, New York, 25 June 2001.
3. All these figures are from *AIDS Epidemic Update 2006*, UNAIDS, December 2006 <www.unaids.org>.
4. Figures from *AIDS Epidemic Update 2006* and *The Female AIDS Epidemic: 2006*, The Global Coalition on Women and AIDS, UNAIDS, 2006.

5.   UNAIDS <www.unaids.org/en/issues/affected_communities/orphans.asp>.

6.   Glynn J.R. et al., 'Why do Young Women Have a Much Higher Prevalence of HIV than Young Men? A Study in Kismu, Kenya and Ndola, Zambia,' in *Journal of Acquired Immune Deficiency Syndromes*, Vol. 15 (Supplement 4) 2003, pp. 851–60 cited in *Facts and Figures on HIV/AIDS*, UNIFEM, July 2004.

7.   Cited in *AIDS Epidemic Update: Women and AIDS*, UNAIDS, December 2004, p. 10.

8.   Dunkle, Kristin L. et al., 2004. 'Gender-based Violence, Relationship Power, and Risk of HIV Infection in Women Attending Ante-natal Clinics in South Africa,' *Lancet*, Vol. 363, No. 9419, cited in *Currents*, November 2004, UNIFEM.

9.   From an interview by Kathambi Kinoti in *Resource Net Friday File*, Issue 205, 3 December 2004, Association for Women's Rights in Development <www.awid.org/go.php?list=analysis&prefix=analysis&item=00218>.

10.   Extract from speech at launch of *I Have a Story to Tell*, CAMFED, 2004, cited in *Learning to Survive: How Education for All Would Save Millions of Young People from HIV/AIDS*, Global Campaign for Education, April 2004, p. 18.

11.   *Policy Paralysis: A Call for Action on HIV/AIDS-Related Human Rights Abuses Against Women and Girls in Africa*, Human Rights Watch, December 2003, p. 30 <www.hrw.org/reports/2003/africa1203/>.

12.   'Zambia: The Ultimate Sacrifice,' *IRIN/PlusNews*, 2004, cited in *Women and HIV/AIDS: Confronting the Crisis*, UNAIDS, United Nations Family Planning Association/United Nations Development Fund for Women (UNIFEM), 2004, p. 23.

13.   *Report on the global AIDS epidemic 2004*, UNAIDS, p. 113 <http://www.unaids.org/bangkok2004/GAR2004_html/GAR2004_00_en.htm>.

14.   *Policy Paralysis: A Call for Action*, p. 40. <http://www.hrw.org/reports/2003/africa1203/5.htm#_Toc56508488>.

15.   *Double Standards: Women's Property Rights Violations in Kenya*, Human Rights Watch, March 2003, p.3.

16.   *Gender-related Socio-economic Impact of HIV/AIDS in Zimbabwe*, UNIFEM, April 2000, p. 14.

17.   Ilene Wong, 'For Poor Women, an AIDS Safety Net,' *Washington Post*, 15 July 2005.

18.   *Gender Equality in AIDS Prevention: Why we need prevention options for women*, Fact Sheet 4, Global Campaign for Microbicides <www.global health.org/images/pdf/public_policy/microbicides_fact4.pdf>.

19.   AIDS Epidemic Update December 2005: Sub-Saharan Africa, p.2 <http://www.unaids.org/en/Regions_Countries/Regions/SubSaharan Africa.asp>.

20. *Policy Paralysis: A Call for Action*, p. 35.
21. Discussion at *Global Challenges to Women's Human Rights Conference*, 9 December 2004, London.
22. J. Vandemoortele and E. Delamonica 'Education "vaccine" against HIV/AIDS,' in *Current Issues in Comparative Education*, Vol. 3 No. 1, cited in *Learning to Survive*, p. 2.
23. *AIDS Epidemic Update*, December 2005: Sub-Saharan Africa, p.2.
24. *Report on the Global HIV/AIDS Epidemic 2000*, UNAIDS/WHO, UNAIDS, Geneva cited in *Learning to Survive*, p. 2.
25. Knut Fylkesnes et al., 'Declining HIV Prevalence and Risk Behaviours in Zambia: Evidence from Surveillance and Population-based Surveys,' in *AIDS*, Vol. 15, 4 May 2001, cited in *HIV & AIDS in Zambia: The Epidemic and its Impact*, Avert <www.avert.org/aids-zambia.htm>.
26. *Learning to Survive, p. 4.*
27. According to *AIDS Epidemic Update 2005*, HIV prevalence rates are also falling in Kenya and Zimbabwe. However, this may be at least partly due to increased death rates.
28. These figures are from *AIDS Epidemic Update December 2006*, UNAIDS/WHO, and *Zambia Summary Country Profile for HIV/AIDS Treatment Scale-up,* WHO/UNAIDS, December 2005. Both cited in *HIV and AIDS in Zambia: The Epidemic and its Impact*, Avert <www.avert.org/aids-zambia.htm>.

Bibliography

This is a list of useful books, although few are written from a specific women's rights perspective. It does not list reports, the details of which are given in the section endnotes, or websites, which are listed separately.

Aikman, S. and Unterhalter, E. (eds), *Beyond Access: Transforming Policy and Practice for Gender Equality in Education*, Oxfam GB, Oxford, 2005.

An-Na'im, A., *Cultural Transformation and Human Rights in Africa*, Zed Books, London and New York, 2002.

Black, M., *The No-Nonsense Guide to Development*, Verso, London, 2002.

Buckman, G., *Global Trade: Past Mistakes, Future Choices*, Zed Books, London and New York, 2005.

Cornwall, A. and Welbourne, A., *Realizing Rights: Transforming Approaches to Sexual Reproductive Well-Being*, Institute of Development Studies, Sussex, UK, 2002.

Dunkley, G., *Free Trade: Myth, Reality and Alternatives*, Zed, London and New York, 2004.

Eade, D. (ed.), *Development and Culture*, Development in Practice Reader, Oxfam GB, London, 2002.

Elson, Diane, Budgeting for Women's Rights: Monitoring Government Budgets for Compliance with CEDAW, UNIFEM. 2006 Available for downloading <www.unifem.org/attachments/products/MonitoringGovernmentBudgetsComplianceCEDAW_eng.pdf>

Ellwood, W., *The No-Nonsense Guide to Globalisation*, Verso, London, 2001.

Gready, P. and Ensor, J. (eds), *Reinventing Development? Translating Rights-based Approaches from Theory into Practice*, Zed, London and New York, 2005.

Kerr, J., Symington, A. and Sprenger, E. (eds), *The Future of Women's Rights: Global Visions and Strategies*, Zed Books, London and New York, 2004.

Masika, R. (ed.), *Gender, Development and Climate Change*, Oxfam GB, 2002.

Molyneux, M. and Razavi, S. (eds.), *Gender Justice, Development and Rights*, Oxford University Press, Oxford, 2002.

Rowlands, J., *Questioning Empowerment: Working with Women in Honduras*, Oxfam, London, 1997.

Ruxton, S. (ed.), *Gender Equality and Men: Learning from Practice*, Oxfam GB, Oxford, 2004.

Seabrook, J., *The No-Nonsense Guide to World Poverty*, Verso, London, 2004.

Seager, J., *The Atlas of Women*, The Women's Press, London, 2003.

Sen, A., *Development as Freedom*, Oxford University Press, Oxford, 1999.

Singh, S., Questioning Globalization, Zed, 2005.

Sweetman, C. (ed.), *Gender in the 21st Century*, Oxfam GB, Oxford, 2000.

Sweetman, C. (ed.), *Gender, Development and Poverty*, Focus on Gender series, Oxfam GB, Oxford, 2002.

Sweetman, C. (ed.), *Gender, Development and Trade*, Oxfam GB, Oxford, 2004.

Usdin, S., *The No-Nonsense Guide to HIV/AIDS*, Verso, London, 2003.

Wichterich, C., *The Globalized Woman: Reports From a Future of Inequality*, Zed, New York, 2000.

Wyn Davies, M. and Sardar, Z., *The No-Nonsense Guide to Islam*, Verso, London, 2004.

Index

A

Abbasgholizadeh, Mahboobeh, 59
ABC strategy, 145–6
abortion, 1, 12–14, 123
    NGO support and global gag rule, 55–6
    see also sex-selective abortion
accountability, 17
ActionAid International, 112, 116, 172
Activa, 38, 39
Adidas, 97–100
adultery, charges of, 61
Afghanistan, 70–4
    US invasion of, 37
Africa, 32–3, 48–50, 89, 102–3, 159
    sub-Saharan, 6–7, 82–3, 117–20, 137–51
    see also individual countries by name
African Charter on Human and Peoples' Rights, 49, 146–7
agricultural work *see* farming
aid, international, 113–14, 145–6
Akpan, Eno-Obong, 45
Ali, Saida, 50
Ames, Patricia, 110
Amnesty International, 34–5, 122, 130–1, 132, 166
Ana Clara, 97
Angola, 87
Annan, Kofi, 32
Antrobus, Peggy, 5–6, 177n5

apartheid, 27
arrests of activists, 59
Asia, 41, 102–3, 133, 138
    factory work in, 92–5, 97–100, 169
    see also individual countries by name
Asociación Aurora Vivar (AVV), 17–18, 21–3, 31, 163, 179n26
Association for Gender and Education (AMME), 112–13
Association for Women's Rights in Development (AWID), 30–1, 81, 152, 163, 167, 175
Atieno, Margaret, 143
Aung San Suu Kyi, 42
awareness-raising, 49, 61
al-Azam, Yousra, 52

B

Balchin, Cassandra, 38, 57, 59–60
Bangladesh, 45, 46–7, 93, 113, 114, 124–5, 133, 158
Baobab for Women's Rights, 39, 59, 61–3, 167–8
barriers to power, four, 70
Basha, Amal, 64
BBC, 163
Begum, Feroze, 78
Begum, Shamim Ara, 134
Beijing Conference *see* World Conference on Women
Beijing Platform for Action (BPFA), 32, 36, 39, 68, 84

Beyond Access Project, 172
Bhutto, Benazir, 57
Bibi, Kulsum, 135
biotechnology, 152–4
Blair, Tony, 5, 6
blogging, 59–60
Bosnia, 26, 121
Botswana, 143
Brazil, 122, 126
British Council, 164
Brown, Gordon, 5
Buerk, Roland, 46
Burma, 42
Bush, President George W., 54, 55,
   157
businesses
   small, 87, 95
   start-ups, 119, 135
Bwiza, Connie, 77

C
Cambodia, 122, 127, 138
Campaign Against Female Foeticide,
   14
Campaign for Female Education
   (CAMFED), 106, 172
   CAMFED Association (CAMA),
   117–20, 139
Canada, 128
CARE-Malawi, 14
caring functions of women, 85, 144,
   145
   see also childcare
Carrion, Doris Solis, 67
Catholics for a Free Choice (CFFC),
   54, 168
Centre for the Study of Violence and
   Reconciliation (South Africa), 137
Centre for Women's Initiatives, 47
charities, 60, 161, 163–76
childbirth, deaths in, 1, 49
childcare provision/responsibilities,
   67, 85, 115, 144

children
   female work in the home, 10–11,
      103, 108, 110, 115, 120, 145
   mortality, 8, 44, 53, 104, 106,
      123, 125
   rights of, 29
   work by, 105, 120, 144–5
Children's Act 2001 (Kenya), 49
Chile, 39, 96–7
China, 43, 92–4, 109, 138, 169
Chinese Working Women Network
   (CWWN), 169
Christian alliance, 56
Christianity, fundamental opposed to
   women's rights, 51–63
Clean Clothes Campaign, 95, 100,
   170
climate change, 9, 157–60
Clinton, President Bill, 55
clothing
   female, 42–3
   Islamic, 58, 61
Coburn, Senator Tom, 55
COICAPEP, 74
Coker-Appiah, Dorcas, 30, 146
coming of age ceremonies, 49, 150
Commission for Africa, 5, 6, 177n3,
   177n4
   women members of, 6
community kitchens, 21–2
Confederation of Voluntary
   Associations (COVA), 75–80
Connor, Timothy, 99–100
consumerism, 12–14
contraception, 155
   Catholic opposition to, 53–4
   clinics and global gag rule, 55–6
   as protection against HIV/AIDS,
      145, 147
Convention against Torture and
   Other Cruel, Inhuman or
   Degrading Treatment or
   Punishment, 132

Convention for the Elimination of
	All Forms of Discrimination
	against Women (CEDAW), 24,
	27–31, 33, 36, 39, 40, 84, 89,
	131, 146, 148
	Article 2, 30
	Article 7, 65
	Article 16, 30
	Optional Protocol, 31, 179n10
	reservations against, 30
	shadow report, 40
Convention on the Rights of the
	Child, 29, 45, 102, 110, 148
co-operatives, 96, 170
conscientisation, 116
corruption, 21
Costa Rica, 65, 66
counselling, 61, 67
Coya, Alejandrina Rosaria Flores, 22
credit, access to, 10, 15, 36, 89
Cuba, 65, 66
cultural activities, 34
cultural relativism, 41–50
Cyrus Cylinder, 27

D
Dairiam, Shanthi, 31, 36
Darfur, 121
Day Chocolate Company, 96, 170
deaths
	infant, 44, 106, 123, 125
	penalty for adultery, 61
	predicted from HIV/AIDS, 53
	in pregnancy and childbirth, 1, 7
	resulting from violence against
		women, 1
Democratic Republic of Congo, 121,
	129–30, 132
Demus, 126–7, 173
Department for International
	Development (DfID) (UK), 15
deregulation, economic, 82–3
development

economic, 8
human, 9
political nature of, 15–17
rights-based approach to, 15–18
Development Alternatives with
	Women for a New Era (DAWN),
	57, 83, 164, 177n5
disasters, natural, 126–9, 157–9
discrimination, 179n1
	affecting poverty, 85–9
	various grounds for, 4
	see also education, human rights,
		work
divorce, 62
domestic work, 11, 85, 145
	by children, 10–11, 103, 108, 110,
		115, 120, 145
dowries, 2, 44, 149
	violence related to, 12–14, 34, 123,
		132–3, 135, 178n14, 180n12
dumping of goods, 20, 81, 90–1

E
East Timor, 109
economic rights of women, 81–100
Ecuador, 67
education, 89, 101–20, 140, 147
	disparity in primary, 6, 102,
		109–10
	disparity in secondary, 6, 106
	fees for, 82, 101, 109, 139, 142,
		144
	inadequate provision of, 108
	poor quality of, 103, 110
	right to, 26
	small-scale NGO initiatives, 115
	women denied, 25, 26, 44, 185n2
Education for All Fast Track
	Initiative (FTI), 113–14
Elson, Diane, 85
empowerment, 4, 6, 11–15, 161–2
	and literacy, 114–17
equity and country wealth, 12

F
fair trade initiatives, 96, 161–2
Family Planning Association (Kenya), 55
famine, 159
farming, 20, 86–8, 90–2, 153, 159
Fawcett Society, 70
Federation of African Women Educationalists (FAWE), 113, 115
female genital mutilation (FGM), 33, 34, 42, 47–50, 60, 123
fertility rates, 125
Foster, Lesley Anne, 40
fostering, 120
Free Legal Aid Committee (India), 2–3
Freire, Paulo, 15, 116
fundamentalism, 51–63, 181n2

G
G7, 7
G8 Gleneagles summit, 5
Gambia, The, 10
Ganbugan Serikat Buruh Independen (GSBI), 98
Gandhi, Indira, 75
Gandhi, Sonia, 75
Garcia, Maria Ysabel Cedano, 128
Gawaya, Rose, 33–4
Genanet, 176
Gender and Development Network (UK), 6
Gender Studies and Human Rights Centre (Ghana), 146
gender audits, 96
genetically modified plants, 153
genital mutilation *see* female genital mutilation
genocide, 76
Ghana, 91, 96, 117, 118, 120, 145, 146
girls' clubs, 115–16

Global Campaign for Education, 107, 113, 148, 173
Global Campaign for Microbicides, 146
Global CEDAW Optional Protocol Campaign, 40
global gag rule, 55–6
global South, definition, 3
global warming, 9, 157–60
globalisation, 45, 46–7, 81–100
    definitions, 82–3
Gonzales, Sandra, 128
Gordon, Gill, 151
Grady, Heather, 19–20, 178n24
Guatemala, 53, 74–5

H
Hamas, 52
Harouna, Waramatou, 107
health and safety at work, 99
health
    consequences of violence, 124
    services, 7, 44, 140, 142–3
HIV/AIDS, 8, 104, 129, 137–51, 173, 175, 190n26
    figures on, 138
    and opposition to contraception, 53–4
    predicted deaths, 53
    prevention methods/programmes, 55, 140
    and violence, 124
    ways forward, 145–8
Hongjiao, Li, 109
hours of work, 10–11, 94–5, 98
human development *see* development, human
human rights, 6, 118, 161
    abuses in families, 35
    abuses by governments, 35
    arguably not suited to Asia, 41
    cultural relativism and, 42–3
    definition, 25–6

enabling, 104
to freedom from violence, 123
international agreements, 3, 26–34
negative, 25
'right to have', 14
to sexuality, 50
'special procedures', 35
training about, 21–2
usefulness questioned, 37
violations, 37–8
women's, 25–40
Human Rights Watch, 35, 72–3,
    141, 166
hurricanes, 157–9

I

illiteracy, 89, 114–17
proportion of women, 1, 101, 103
see also literacy, training
Imam, Ayesha, 61–3
imprisonment, 98
India, 2–3, 12–15, 27, 36, 42, 75,
    114, 115, 117, 118, 138
caste system, 26
female political representation,
    75–80
violence against women, 12–14,
    125–6, 132–3
Indonesia, 97–100
industrial action, 98
informal economic sector, 85–6, 97
inheritance, laws on, 56, 88–9, 123,
    140, 146
see also land ownership
Institute of Education, 172
International Conference on
    Population and Development
    1994, 29, 50, 52
International Covenant on Civil and
    Political Rights (ICCPR), 28
International Covenant on
    Economic, Social and Cultural
    Rights (ICESR), 28, 84

International Criminal Court, 121, 132
International Day for the Elimination
    of Violence against Women, 129
International Gender and Trade
    Network, 95, 170
International HIV/AIDS Alliance,
    148, 151, 175
International Labour Organization
    (ILO), 84, 93, 183n4
International Monetary Fund (IMF),
    83
International Planned Parenthood
    Federation, 55
International Women's Rights Action
    Watch, 31
Inter–Parliamentary Union, 169
in-vitro fertilisation (IVF), 154, 156
Iran, 53, 59
Iraq
constitution and Sharia law, 56
war in, 37
Islam, 51–63, 115, 168

J

Jain, Devaki, 38
Jalal, Masouda, 73
Jena, Esther, 101
jobs *see* work
Jyoti Sangh, 132–3

K

Kabeer, Naila, 14–15
Kandiyoti, Deniz, 43
Kapenza, Yvonne, 120
Karzai, Hamid, 71
Katrina, Hurricane, 157–8
Kaufman, Michael, 128–9
Kenya, 47–9, 55, 109, 141, 144,
    190n26
Khatoon, Jamal, 11, 25
Khatun, Ayesha, 46
Kinoti, Kathambi, 32, 50
Kuapa Kokoo, 96, 170

L
labour
  rights, 93–4
  sexual division of, 10
  see also work
Labour Behind the Label, 95
land ownership rights, 10, 42, 88–9,
  92, 142, 143
Latin America, 15, 31–2, 54
  see also individual countries by
  name
Lawal, Amina, 62–3
Lee Kuan Yew, 41
legislation
  on abuse of students, 113
  on domestic violence, 146
  on divorce, 140
  on equality, 40
  on inheritance, 56, 88–9, 123, 140,
  146
  prohibiting FGM, 49
  on human rights, 3, 38, 39–40, 45
  Sharia law, 56–7, 59, 61–3, 168
  on working conditions, 95
letter-writing campaigns, 62–3
literacy, 15, 16, 69, 73, 101, 114–17,
  147
  Reflect approach, 116, 118
  see also illiteracy
Livingstone, Ken, 124
Lopez, Isabel Gregoria Garcia, 74–5
Lukindo, Vumiliar, 130–1

M
Maendeleo Ya Wanawake (MYWO),
  49
Magazu, Bariya, 62
Make Poverty History, 7, 19
Make Trade Fair, 19, 125, 161
Makhi Welfare Organisation, 115
malaria, 8, 104
Malawi, 109, 113
Mali, 69–70

marriage, early, 30, 106–8, 112, 140,
  149, 150
  in Nigeria, 44–5
Martens, Jackie, 130
Masimanyane Women's Support
  Centre, 38–9, 40, 164, 173
Mawardi, Ngadineh Binti Abu, 98
medical tourism, 156
Mexico, 91–2, 126
micro-credit, 15, 36
microbicides, 145–6
migrants, 42, 98
military spending, 114
Millennium Development Goals,
  5–7, 8, 18, 39, 103–4, 106
  MDG2, 104
  MDG3, 6–7, 18, 103–4, 172
  MDG5, 7
Mitch, Hurricane, 158–9
Mobile Crèches, 115
Mogae, Festus, 137
Mohamad, Mahathir, 41
mothers, young, *see* pregnancy of
  young girls
Mozambique, 65, 66, 93, 112–13
Mugwendere, Aneline, 139, 142
Mukagabiro, Grace, 76
Mukhopadhyay, Maitrayee, 47, 48
Mulia, Siti Musdah, 57–8
Muna, Jagyaseni, 118
murder of women by men, 127–8,
  132–3
Muslim Council of Britain, 60
Muslims, 51, 56–7, 70, 168
  community in the UK, 42–3, 60
  in India, 77–8
  women, 56–7
  see also Islam
Mutekezda, Chief, 119–20

N
neo-liberalism, 82
Nepal, 16, 133–4, 178n22

Nicaragua, 122
Niger, 107, 159
Nigeria, 26, 59, 61–3, 104–5, 110,
    167–8
  corruption in, 114
  early marriage in, 44–5
  out of school children, 105
Nike, 93, 98
Nirantar, 116–17
non-governmental organizations
    (NGOs), 14–15, 77, 96, 163–76
  funding and global gag rule, 55–6
  see also individual NGOs by name
North American Free Trade
    Agreement (NAFTA), 91–2
N'Soma, Adelina, 87

O
Ojha, Bishnu, 16
Oeuvre malienne d'aide à la femme
    et à l'enfant (OMAFES), 69
Organization for Economic
    Co-operation and Development
    (OECD), 100
Owimana, Yvonne, 77
Owino, Emily, 144
Oxfam, 7, 125, 161, 164–5
  aid activities of, 11, 16, 97
  Australia, 98–9, 170
  campaigns, 33, 68, 90, 96, 126
  Great Britain, 164, 172
  policies of, 4, 15, 83, 95, 123
  and rights-based approach, 19–20
  staff, 33, 76, 88, 135–6

P
Paez, Erika, 22–3
Pakistan, 11, 57, 59, 71, 111, 114,
    115, 133
Pandey, Santosh, 134–5
Panos Institute, 165
parliamentary representation, 21, 57,
    64–80, 182n1
  in Afghanistan, 71–4
  proportion of, 1, 64, 66
  quota systems, 72–3, 75, 78,
    183n13
PATH, 48, 49, 167
Pathan, Zarmeena, 74
pay
  low, 98
  unequal, 36, 86, 88
Peru, 20–3, 93, 110, 127–8
Planned Parenthood Association
    (Zambia), 148
political activity of women, 64–80,
    118
  in Afghanistan, 71–4
  in India, 75–80
  as proxies for men, 78
  in Rwanda, 76–7
  see also parliamentary representa-
    tion
Polli Sree, 134
Pope Benedict XVI, 53–4
population, proportion of women, 1,
    13–14
Population Action, 55
Population Services International
    (PSI), 55
poverty, 149
  affected by discrimination, 85–9
  crusade to end world, 5
  and education, 107–8
  in Mexico, 92
  in Peru, 21
  proportions living in, 82–3
  voice poverty, 68
  women as major sufferers of, 1,
    5–8, 83
  working poor, 86
  World Bank definition, 8
power
  and education, 117
  inequalities in, 12, 15, 47, 153
  political see political activity of

women, parliamentary
    representation
pregnancy,
  deaths in, 1
  of young girls, 44, 53, 105, 108,
    112–13, 150
Prevention of Witch Practices Act
    (India), 2
privatisation, 82–3
Programme H, 126
Project Against Domestic Violence
    (Cambodia), 126–7, 173
Protocol on the Rights of Women in
    Africa, 32–3
PT Panarub, 97–100
purdah, 45, 46, 158

R
racism, 51
Rai, Usha, 14
Rajkotia, Malavika, 13
rape, 26, 112, 128, 135
  in wartime, 121, 130–1
  and Sharia law, 61
Reagan, President Ronald, 55
registration of birth, 74–5
Rehman, Maulana Hift ur-, 71
religious issues, 51–63
reproductive technology, 154–5
Respect, 60
rights see human rights
rituals
  coming of age, 49, 150
  FGM as, 48–9
Robinson, Mary, 24
Röhr, Ulrike, 152, 157–60
role models, 105, 108
  lack of, 111
Royal Tropical Institute, 169
Rwanda, 26, 65, 66, 75, 76–7, 147

S
Sachs, Albie, 41, 43

Sahel region, 20
Samson, Ann Elisabeth, 152–6
Sarpong, June, 91
Saudi Arabia, 65
Save the Children, 106
Seaweed Collectors' Union, Chile, 97
Seed Money Scheme, 119
self-esteem, 9, 101
  and education, 110
Sen, Amartya, 9, 26, 125
sex-selective abortion, 1, 12–14, 123,
    133, 155, 160–1
sex workers, 125, 139, 145, 149,
    178n22
sexual abuse, 112–13, 119, 150
sexual activity, 149–50
'sexual cleansing', 144
sexual harassment, 26, 123, 125,
    150
  in schools/colleges, 101, 103, 108,
    111, 112–13, 134–5, 147
  at work, 125
Sharia law, 56–7, 59, 61–3, 168
Sharma, Nisha, 13
Shefali, Mashuda Khatun, 46–7
shelters for abused women, 67
Simpson, Tim, 56
Sisters' Arabic Forum, 64
Sivanesan, Shanthi, 135–6
small businesses, 87, 95, 119, 135
social floor, 84
Social Information and Legal
    Guidance Foundation, 100
Social Watch, 12, 171
Solidarity for African Women's
    Rights, 33
Souko, Keita Kendja, 69–70
South Africa, 27, 34, 40, 41, 86–8,
    137, 139, 141, 145, 164
  Women's Budget Initiative, 96
Sow, Fatou, 56–7
Sri Lanka, 135–6, 159
Stacey, Maree, 43

stereotypes, negative, 103, 111
street-portering, 120
structural adjustment, 20, 82–3
subsidies for agriculture, 90–1
'sugar daddies', 139, 140, 142, 145
sustainability, 8, 169

T
Taller de Acción Cultural, 97
Tanzania, 109, 115
teachers
   abuse by, 112–13
   tendency to favour boys, 111
   untrained/inadequate, 108, 110
technology, new, 152–6
terrorism, 51, 57–59
   see also 'War on Terror'
Thailand, 138, 148
Thakker, Manisha, 132–3
Thatcher, Margaret, 67
Tibet, refugee communities, 42
Togo, 33
Togola, Baba, 69
trade
   liberalisation of, 81, 83–100
   unions, 93, 98–100, 171
trafficking in women, 2, 123, 133,
      178n22
training
   in assertiveness, 149–50
   for business start–up, 119
   on human rights, 39
   in literacy, 16, 69, 105, 116–17
   in political activity, 78–9
   in skills, 15, 21
   see also education
Tsikata, Dodzi, 36–7
tsunami (2004), 126, 135–6, 157–8

U
Uganda, 109, 122, 126, 143, 146,
      148
United Kingdom, 6, 65, 83

Bradford, 42
   domestic violence in, 124
   Muslim community, 42–3, 60
   women's suffrage movement, 65
United Nations (UN), 5, 27, 123, 169
   Development Fund for Women
      (UNIFEM), 68, 165
   Development Programme (UNDP),
      9
   Division for the Advancement of
      Women, 30
   Educational Scientific and Cultural
      Organization (UNESCO), 114
   Emergency Fund for Children
      (UNICEF), 124, 173
   High Commissioner for Human
      Rights, 35, 166
   Human Rights Council, 27
   Joint Programme on HIV/AIDS
      (UNAIDS), 138, 175
United States, 65, 132, 151
   economic policies, 83
   farm subsidies and dumping, 90–1
   human rights violations, 37–8
   and Hurricane Katrina, 157–8
   USAID, 145–6
United Students Against Sweatshops,
      96
Universal Declaration of Human
      Rights (UDHR), 25, 27, 28, 102,
      166
   Article 2, 27
   Article 5, 34–5

V
vesico-vaginal fistulae (VVF), 44–5
Viagra, 153
VIE, 107
Vietnam, 89
violence against women, 1, 10, 34,
      35, 121–36, 139, 140, 173–4
   definitions, 123
   domestic, 14, 122

dowry–related, 12–14
and HIV/AIDS, 139, 141
right not to endure, 25
sexual, 35 (see also rape)
during wars, 129–30
voice poverty, 68
vote
registration to, 71–2
right to, 27, 57, 65

W
Wanjala, Monique, 139, 141
'War on Terror', 37–8, 57–9
wars, 129–30, 132
water
scarcity, 159–60
work to fetch, 11, 118
We Are Not Machines, 98, 100
'We Can' campaign, 126, 133–5,
174, 177n2
Welsh Assembly, 70
White Ribbon Campaign (WRC), 26,
126, 128–9, 174
WHRnet, 167
widows, 33, 123, 140, 143
wife inheritance, 140, 143–4
Win, Everjoice, 17–18
'witch hunts', 2
WOMANKIND Worldwide, 22–3,
165–6, 177n1
Women Against Fundamentalisms,
51, 53, 168
Women in Development Europe
(WIDE), 83, 95, 171
Women Fighting Aids, 141
Women Living Under Muslim Laws
(WLUML), 57, 168
Women Working Worldwide, 95–6,
171
Women's Edge Coalition, 95, 171
Women's Environment and
Development Organisation, 32
Women's India Association, 27

Women's Skill Creation Centre
(Nepal), 16
Wong, Ilene, 145
work, 183n4
in Asian factories, 92–5, 97–100,
169
banned under the Taliban, 73
career aspirations, 105
by children, 105, 120, 144–5
conditions of, 94–5, 97–100, 170,
171
created through globalisation,
45–7, 84, 86, 92–5
domestic see domestic work
informal, 85–6, 97
precarious nature of, 23, 92
sex-segregated, 96
sexual harassment at, 125
traditional spheres of women's, 86
unpaid, 85
and violence, 124–5
Work, Women and Economy, 22
Worker Rights Consortium (WRC),
99, 171–2
World Bank, 8, 14, 23, 83, 109, 124,
177n11
World Conference on Human Rights
1993, 29
World Conference on Women
(Beijing), 29, 32, 50, 60
World Education Forum, 116
World Health Organization, 54, 121,
124, 174
World Summit 2005, 7, 32, 103
World Trade Organization (WTO),
20, 83, 90, 95

Z
Zambia, 14, 33–4, 117, 141, 142,
147, 148–51
Zimbabwe, 106, 117, 145, 190n26